Shetland's Open Boat Days

Shetland's Open Boat Days
Tales of the fishing under sail and oar

By
TOM HENDERSON
CHARLES JOHNSON
JAMES J. LAURENSON
WILLIAM NICOLSON

Edited by Charlie Simpson

The Shetland Times Ltd.
Lerwick
2017

Shetland's Open Boat Days

First published by The Shetland Times Ltd., 2017.

ISBN 978-1-910997-13-0

British Library Cataloguing-in-Publication Data
A catalogue record for this book is available from the British Library

Thanks to the generosity of the copyright owners royalties from the sale of this book will go to support Shetland Boat Week.

Printed and published by
The Shetland Times Ltd.,
Gremista, Lerwick,
Shetland, Scotland. ZE1 0PX

Dedicated with great respect to Duncan Sandison of Baltasound, now in the tenth decade of a life dedicated to the preservation of Shetland's open boat tradition in all its many and various forms.

Contents

Foreword

150 years ago fishing in six-oared boats, miles offshore, was a mainstay of the Shetland economy, and the norm in peripheral parts of the islands. Nowadays there is not much physical evidence of the boats or their equipment, and accounts of the fishery, especially by participants, have become difficult to find.

Now Charlie Simpson has brought together some fine narratives of Shetland's haaf fishing era and its disasters. The authors were expert in the subject, either from personal experience, or from deep knowledge of their communities' history. Some of them were very fine stylists, even when – like Charles Johnson – they had no former experience of prose-writing. Their accounts span the final seven decades of the nineteenth century.

Tom Henderson combined local knowledge with a supple writing style. His account of "The night that Mouat was lost", in Shetland dialect, the result of deep discussion with his father, is a classic of Shetland literature.

Charles Johnson's recreation of his night on the brink of disaster in 1881, told calmly – "I had been brought up with boating since I was a child, but this of course was a bit extra" – is a masterpiece.

Jeemsie Laurenson, an institution in his native island of Fetlar, preserves incidents, and even conversations from the same dire night: and Willie Nicholson's eye-witness account of another tempest, in 1900, recorded half a century ago, completes the volume.

The fishermen who made their living in small open boats around Shetland became experts in reading the sea and sky. Few of them wrote about their working lives. Charlie Simpson's collection of the best accounts makes the day-to-day experiences and dramas of the haaf fishing period available to a new generation.

Brian Smith
Shetland Archives

Introduction

'Our open boat under sail is a thing alive
and only needs proper guidance'
– Charles Johnson

Shetland has always been, and forever will be, a place where boats are valued. Today, they're not as essential to life as they once were, and far fewer of us use them to make a living, but in every sheltered inlet from Norwick to Fair Isle, Foula to Bressay, you'll find a boat of some kind nearby. When once there were only wooden boats, oars and sails, today there are many ways of going afloat to enjoy a wide range of watery pursuits, be it in the *Swan* or a kayak – and all manner of craft in between.

Whatever the craft, there's more or less a universal respect for the sea and its moods. There's also a widespread interest in the tools our forefathers used to make their precarious living; how they developed their boats and their gear, and how they were used, especially in the haaf fisheries of the open ocean.

While there are still a good number of people of my generation who went fishing in wooden fourareens under sail or oar, we went for sport, not a living. The days of the vocational open boat fisheries are history now, and beyond living memory. Few of us were fortunate enough to absorb old men's tales when we were young, and so now the only available sources of information on the era are those in print or – extremely rarely – on recording tape. There's a multitude of contributions in this field, to be sure, but it's nearly all contained in out-of-print books and periodicals, or in newspaper archives and old official records. In some respects, the boats endured longer than the men, for there are several post-war publications based mainly on reminiscences of old boat-builders and measurements of a few decaying hulls. We're fortunate, though, that the tales of many of those who actually used the boats through the latter part of the era were written down by attentive listeners, and even more fortunate in that at least one haaf fishermen was able to do it himself, and write of his calling toward the end of his life.

The idea for this book came one day when Brian Smith happened to mention that a similar publication project had come to nothing a dozen years ago. He had just found for me a newspaper article involving a storm of 1887, which turned out to have been written, not by a reporter, but a fisherman at sea on the day. Our discussion shifted to literary merit, and concluded with the realisation that this might be a good time to restore some of this body of boating and fishing lore to the public domain. After much deliberation, we decided to concentrate on our three favourite writers on the subject: one who was actually there and two who combined their memories of the tales of their elders with intelligent research. To this, we have added the edited transcript of the words of one who survived the appalling disaster in 1900 that befell the fishermen of Delting, a story that appears in print for the first time. (Apart from the latter tale, the others remain as written, with only a word of explanation added here and there in square brackets). The pieces begin with an overview of the boats, then follow a reasonably chronological path through the history of the fisheries that, along with the tales of disastrous events, sheds much light on the day-to-day working life of the open boat fishermen. Their lives were so far removed from our power-driven existence today as to be almost unimaginable, yet for centuries their drive powered the economic engine whose continuation has kept our islands successfully in business right to the present day, while from them, far more of us are descended than we perhaps realise.

Acknowledgments

This publication could not have proceeded without the willing approval of the copyright holders of the original material. Grateful thanks for their consent are therefore due to Mrs Ann Mouat of Invercargill, New Zealand, for the stories of her uncle Tom Henderson, Robert Johnson of East Voe, Scalloway, for those of his grandfather Charles Johnson, Mrs Laureene Pottinger-Donald of Leith, Edinburgh, for those of her grand-uncle Jeemsie Laurenson and Mrs Maureen Cumming of Uphouse, Ollaberry for the epic tale of her grandfather William Nicolson. Their generosity means that a payment of ten percent of retail sales of this book will go towards the running costs of Shetland Boat Week in future years.

The assistance of Brian Smith and Angus Johnson of Shetland Museum and Archives was a crucial element of the project in the selection and supply of texts and is much appreciated.

Tom Henderson

Tom Henderson.
Shetland Museum and Archives

Tom Henderson M.B.E. was born at Spiggie in 1911. He was a pupil at Boddam school , and went to sea at the age of 19. He married in 1938 and came ashore, but went back to sea when war broke out. In 1941 his ship was torpedoed off the West African coast and Tom survived but seriously injured his back. He became paralysed below the waist, and spent 3½ years flat on his back, in a plaster cast, before he recovered. During this time he was able to write, and produced articles and stories of high quality – mainly with a nautical flavour – for many national periodicals and magazines.

Tom and his wife Kitty ran the Spiggie Hotel for many years, and he had a long career on many public bodies including three years as County Convener. He is probably best remembered today for his fourteen years as Curator of Lerwick Museum from 1966 to 1980, his achievements in safeguarding historical shipwrecks, and his encyclopedic knowledge of all matters nautical that was freely shared and regularly reflected in his writings on local maritime history. He died in 1982.

THE YOAL AND THE SIXERN

(*The New Shetlander.* Nos. 89 and 91, 1969)

For some peculiar reason, the subject of Shetland boat design has over the years become controversial. On the one hand there are the partisans who, in certain cases, have gone so far as to say that the traditional pattern was brought to such a degree of perfection several hundred years ago that since then no improvement has been possible. The Shetland boat has no stauncher champion than I, but this argument I just do not understand. It is true that our oldest Shetland boat type, the Ness or Fair Isle yoal, has changed hardly at all over several centuries; but the sixern, the boat of the far haaf – the deep sea – was a comparatively modern production when one talks in terms of centuries.

She was evolved after the middle of the 18th century to meet the changing needs of the Shetland fishing, and she was still being developed when the haaf fishing came to an end after 1900. Certainly, there is no doubt in my mind that the yoal was the true progenitor of the sixern. Whether, as Charles Sandison would have us believe, the sixern sprang full-fledged from some Shetland designer's brain, or whether – as I am inclined to think – the one design was gradually evolved from the other, the influence of the yoal model on the larger craft is not to be denied. But between the slender hull of the yoal and the deeper, fuller hull of the later sixern there is a world of difference.

On the other side of the argument there are those people who, knowing Shetland boats only as blue-prints on paper, as plates in old books, or as inert hulls standing on beaches, condemn them as dangerous and crank, their only virtue the skill of the men who manned them. Here, of course, it is a question of mere ignorance. It is not from the shore that one can judge the qualities of a boat. You have to be "fram" – well off-shore – with the weather growing and the sea rising by the minute, when the land is dim to leeward and between it and you there is a welter of hissing crests through which you must choose your path – it is then, and only under such circumstances, that you truly come to appreciate how much more went into the fashioning of a yoal's frail fabric than can ever appear in plan or picture.

The Ness Yoal

The boat nowadays called a Ness yoal was once the universal fishing craft of Shetland. As she is certainly one of the most ancient boat types surviving round the coast of Great Britain today, she must also surely be one of the most conservative craft afloat. Not only are her proportions constant, she must also conform within inches to a certain standard measurement which must have been laid down in remote antiquity. She measures 15 feet between the "skaers" (or scarves) of the keel, 21.5 feet over the stems, 5.5 feet in amidships beam, and her inside depth is 21 inches. Add a foot to this overall measurement, or subtract a foot, and men of Dunrossness will tell you that, though she is still probably a good boat she is no longer a yoal. She is a beautiful boat, with a sweeping sheer – which means that she is high at both ends and low in the middle – and flowing, graceful lines which one does not need to be a seaman to admire. Clinker built, her framing is incredibly light. She is a mere shell, and so supple that when standing on a beach, by shaking her stem you can make the other horn oscillate backwards and forwards at least six inches.

A person accustomed to a stiffer, more orthodox craft must view such a boat with deep suspicion. And they do! I have heard a yoal compared to a basket or a "kishie!" But, as any old yoal seaman will tell you, in this resilience and elasticity lies the boat's greatest virtue. This is the factor which cannot appear in blue-print or plan. This is the thing that has to be experienced to be fully understood. Even Charles Sandison, as great an authority on boats as he undoubtedly was, while he realised that this factor was not accidental, believed that the boat had been designed this way to give her added speed. No doubt it does help her speed, but that is not the point. It is the ready give of the Ness yoal's supple hull which makes her the sea-kindly boat she is in rough water.

A yoal has three thwarts, and rows six oars, each man of her crew pulling a pair. Her mast steps through the midship thwart and her sail is almost a true square-sail, set "flying," which means that it is set outside the rigging. Such a sail has tremendous lifting power, and a deep-laden yoal will lift her bow a hand's breadth to the upward pull of her sail. For somewhere the impression has gone abroad that a yoal could only sail before the wind. This is complete nonsense. While she can never be as weatherly as a deeper, heavier craft, a yoal can be sailed close-hauled very effectively and it was the common practice to do so. The fishermen of my boyhood used to drive them unmercifully when on a wind. They thought nothing of laying them down till a midship thole was tearing in the froth – and I would add here that they had no fear whatever of lee water, unless in a string of tide when a sea might break in any direction. It was the "wadder lump", the windward sea, they dreaded and being pooped by a breaking crest when running.

Evolution Of The Sixern

The earliest mention in print of Shetland boats and fishing that I have been able to discover is the account published by Captain John Smith who, on behalf of the Earl of Pembroke, made an exploratory voyage to the islands in 1633. He seems to have found a veritable Mecca for both fisherman and merchant. Fish were to be caught in fantastic numbers close inshore and even in the voes. Having set up a staple [market place] in the island of Unst, he freighted his vessel full in seven weeks trading. Moreover he estimated that, with five Hanseatic merchants operating at the same time, he had only about one-fifth of the total catch landed at Unst. For a fishing of this type, the light yoal was the ideal craft.

But not so long after Smith's visit the pattern changed. About 1680, when various reverend gentlemen in Shetland supplied Sibbald with the papers from which his "Description" is compiled, they speak of the fishing as being "greatly decayed." Brand, writing of what he saw in 1700, uses precisely the same expression. The fish had left the comfortable inshore grounds and were only to be found far to sea. Some writers of the period blame the Dutch herring-fleet which, they claim, by gutting their catches on board and dumping the offal, had attracted the fish away from the land. To modern minds, it seems much more likely that some climactic change was responsible, perhaps a fluctuation in the course of the Gulf Stream which raised the temperature of the shallower seas and sent the fish seeking the chill depths of the open ocean. Whatever the cause, the fish had drawn off the land, never to return, and since where the fish are found, there the fisherman must go. Shetlanders had to put their slender yoals to a trade for which they were never built.

They appear to have been curiously slow to adapt their methods to the new conditions. Right through the first half of the 18th century they certainly persisted with the old type of boat. All the writers of the time mention the constant and increased danger of the fishery – and since this was the age of the pamphleteer, references are not lacking. Even now fishermen are proverbially slow to adopt new ways, yet it seems odd that as late as 1750 the yoal was still the universal boat of the islands, even though, as Brand says, the fishing grounds were so far off "that they almost sink the land." About the middle of the century an experiment was tried of having an escorting sloop with three or four yoals. This was a time-honoured method in other parts of the world, notably on the Grand Banks, but in Shetland it was not a success. The yoals were too big and the mother ship generally too small. In the sort of weather when aid was really needed, the sloop could not lift her boats on board, and the best she could make of it was to take the men out of the boats and let them go.

Sooner or later a larger boat has to be adopted and it is astounding that the change was so long delayed. Not until George Low wrote in 1774 is there any indication of the advent of any larger craft. Describing Northmaven as one of the most important fishing stations in Shetland – which it was – he goes on to say that "here they have the largest boats and venture farthest to sea of all the others..." Those boats, he says, are full 18 feet keel and eight feet of beam.

One would like to know more about the larger boats that Low saw. Were they merely overgrown yoals or had the metamorphosis of the model already begun? Were they built in Shetland or – like the yoals – were they prefabricated in Norway? Charles Sandison, whose opinions are based on sound knowledge, believes that these were still Norwegian-built craft, larger, but adhering closely to the traditional model. He would hail the sixern as an entirely Shetland conception of a later period. I cannot quite accept this. Most of the boats were certainly still built in Norway. But my own researches have forced me to the conclusion that at the time of the disastrous gale of 1791 there were two distinct classes of haaf-boat in use. There was a lighter type of about 17 feet to 18 feet of keel which was considered obsolete and old-fashioned: and there was a deeper, heavier boat that I can only conclude to have been the first clearly-defined step away from the old pattern towards the new.

Yet I have to confess that the earliest set of contemporary measurements that I have found of what is described as "a representative sixern of the old time," dating from 1817, are still not far from the proportions of a very large Ness yoal. This boat was a very famous craft indeed. She was built for Thomas Edmondston of Buness, a naturalist of no mean order, who recorded much relating to birds and the ocean fauna of Shetland. Called the *Haaf Fish* this was the boat used in these studies, but she was an ordinary working sixern for all that. She was 18 feet of keel, 28 feet over the stems, 6 feet 8 inches of beam, and 27 inches of inside depth amidships. She is described as having a very flat floor and a full bottom, and only drawing 14 inches of water with her crew and lines on board.

For a very long time after this, while sixerns became fuller and deeper, their overall length increased very little. And for a very good reason. The old haaf-fishing method involved hauling the boat on a beach during bad weather and when the crew left the haaf station for their homes at the weekend. This imposed a limitation on size which was not exceeded until almost at the very end of the industry. Hibbert mentions sixerns of 20 feet of keel in 1819, and until about 1890 very few exceeded 21 feet. At that time a larger class came in which, unless under the most abnormal circumstances, were left at anchor. The first of these larger boats to come to my own district of Dunrossness was the *Anchor of Hope* owned by my paternal grandfather and skippered by my mother's brother. She was 23 feet of keel and was the subject of a good deal of caustic local comment at the time, her size being attributed – perhaps with some justification – to her skipper's desire to have the biggest yet! But she was a most successful boat and within a few years had been superseded by several Ness sixerns which were even larger, measuring 24 feet on the keel. What I believe to have been the last fishing sixern and the largest of the type ever built in Shetland was also a Dunrossness boat. She was the *Hope*

The replica Unst sixern *Far Haaf* at sea. *Photo by Charlie Simpson*

built for the Irvine brothers of South Voe in 1907 and she measured 27 feet. I remember her well and a fine craft she was; but she was partly decked and rigged with a standing lug and jib, and was therefore no true sixern.

During all this long period of changing conditions the old Shetland yoal lingered on, though in time she was so confined to two districts of Shetland that now she is only spoken of as a Ness or a Fair Isle yoal. There was nothing odd about this. The main fishing both at the Isle and at south Dunrossness was for saithe, a fish of the tearing tide-rousts from which in olden days Dunrossness took its name. No craft ever fashioned by the hand of man was better suited to this turbulent inshore fishing than the yoal; and so, when so much has changed, the yoal is still with us in almost exactly the same form which 17th century writers knew. From about 1850 they ceased to be imported from Norway. A duty on manufactured foreign timber made it cheaper to build them at home. And they are still being built. One or two new ones have appeared in recent years. The proportions and the model remain the same, but where the Norwegian-built boats had five strakes from keel to gunwale, Shetland-built boats have six.

Of recent years we have heard much of the great fishing disasters of 1832 and 1881. Whenever the Shetland sixern comes under discussion these occasions are brought forward as proof of her vulnerability in bad weather. In 1832, 17 boats and over a hundred fishermen were lost; in 1881 the numbers were fewer but serious enough still.

An analysis of what happened at both these times does not, to my mind, score so heavily against the boats after all. On both occasions the haaf-fleet were caught far off the land. It would be less than right to say that the wind came entirely without warning, That can never happen. But anyone who knows the northern seas in summer and who has any knowledge of weather-lore, knows that there is a period from the middle of June onwards when ordinary weather portents seem to be completely awry. That particular appearance of the sky called in Shetland a "weather-head," when it stands from east to west at any other time of the year, means wind and plenty of it before morning. Yet in midsummer it will appear vividly for perhaps three days in succession and nothing worse will come out of it than a shower of rain. "Never trust a July sky," runs the Shetland saying. Thus I have no doubt that the weatherwise haaf-men saw the signs, but being merely a summer sky they ignored them and hoped for the best.

In the 1832 gale, the wind came like a thunderclap at midnight on Monday, the 16th of June, such a wind as no one living had ever known in the summer-time before. It blew without a break until the following Saturday, five days of heart-breaking anxiety and bitter sorrow which will never be forgotten in Shetland. Many boats made the land unaided, though it has been said that not one North Isles sixern fetched north of the Bard of Bressay. Many crews were rescued by Dutch herring-busses and other craft. At least one boat reached Norway, while the crew of another were taken out of her over 100 miles south-east of Fair Isle. It was said that others could have been rescued, but believing that a summer gale must soon blow over, they refused to abandon their boats. This was no ordinary summer gale. It was a cataclysm of nature, fortunately without parallel in the history of the islands. Exposed to the full fury of it, no open boat could do otherwise than run, or head the sea, pulling to windward. Hour after hour, day after day, long before the wind broke men must have been fainting with hunger and fatigue. It would be then that the sea took them.

The gale of 1881 came as suddenly but it only lasted a short time. By next morning it was virtually over. The boats which were lost were fishing north-west from Ronas Hill on the "edge of the deep water," the Great Continental Shelf. It was not the storm alone they had to face, it was coming down on the land in the darkness and the spray, unable to choose their landfall. In Charles Johnson's fine account of that night, he stresses the anxiety on board his own boat before they identified the first land they sighted to be the stack called the Ossa. Another boat made a bad shot for Ronas Voe and met her doom on the Okran Heads. The fate of two others, East Yell boats from the Gloup station, is tied up with one of the most dramatic incidents of the gale.

Three sixerns; a Yell boat, one from Mossbank, and another from Uyea in Northmavine came down the west side of Fethaland together. Fethaland is almost an island, a high lump of land joined to the main by a low neck where was the fishing station. The bays formed on each side of this peninsula are the East and West Wicks of Fethaland. The East Wick is roomy, with a smooth shingle beach. The West Ayre is narrow, with a high stack called Buskie in the throat of it and the beach is steep and rough. Strung out off the nose of the Isle of Fethaland lie the forbidding rocks called the Ramna Stacks.

This was the landfall the three sixerns made, fleeing before the storm: looming rocks and frothing breakers close on board on every hand. No wonder the two strangers flinched from it and bore up to weather the Stacks. But the Uyea man, sure of his ground and trusting in his boat, never hesitated. "Button your jackets, boys," he growled, and laid her fair for the West Ayre. A great sea lifted under them and they eased the sail to let the sixern drop behind the crest. Then they gave her the "cloot" again and cleated the halliards. The time for the towsman's artistry was by. That sea broke in one thundering line of froth from Fethaland to the Ramna Stacks. It completely covered Buskie.

The West Ayre of Fethaland, scene of a dramatic landfall in the great gale of 1881. The sea "broke in one thundering line of froth from Fethaland to the Ramna Stacks" (seen in the distance). *Photo by Alastair Christie-Johnston*

And lifting, flying, on the back of it the Uyea boat came in like a thunderbolt, till she brought up all standing on the head of the West Ayre with her bow in the grass and twenty men snatching at her gunwales to drag her clear of the wash. That same sea ended the Gloup boat, battling her way round the Stacks.

Can anyone say that a boat lost under such conditions needed to be in any way inferior? If those boats had had sea-room under their lee, the outcome would not have been as tragic as it was; and as proof of that let me say that the sixerns fishing off Northmavine were not the only boats at sea that night. There were sixerns off-shore all along the east side of Shetland; and not only did these make port, they beat up to the land under close reefs in the teeth of the storm, the very thing which Omond, writing only a year later, declared that a sixern could not do.

A boat which my family later owned, the Ness sixern *Foam* of Voe, suffered serious damage at the very start. Like the rest of the Ness fleet, she was lying to her bait nets when the wind came, and like the rest her crew cut away the gear and made sail. Plunging heavily before she gathered way, the "Foam" struck into a cresting sea and split a "hassin" [plank] on one side. Immediately she began to fill. With the strain and pressure of her passage, they could not keep the water down. In this moment of crisis young Lowrie Cheyne, the skipper's son, snatched up a ling and a splitting knife, ripped out the backbone and clapped the split fish over the crack. From there all the way up to the land he sat with his boot-soles on top of the fish and his back to the boat's other side, and so they could keep her [dry] with the scoops.

One last story of what a sixern and her crew would survive, and I am done. This was a Stenness sixern and her skipper's name was Manson. She was running for the land on a wild morning, with the sea breaking short and steep as the water shoaled. Wave after wave her skipper had run, easing along to the weaker tails, the towsmen plying the sail as need demanded, the scoop going but keeping the boat dry. Suddenly, too near to dodge, too high to outrun, a great sea lifted and broke on board over both quarters. It not only filled the sixern to the thwarts, which many a boat has survived: it filled her to the very brim. If she had had stone ballast instead of fish on board, she would have sunk like a stone. As it was she lay dead in the water for moments, her dazed crew sitting like statues on the thwarts, the sea swilling across both gunwales amidships. The towsman was fumbling to get the sail off when suddenly the skipper barked: "Keep dat cloot staundin!" Through his boots he had felt life in her. Then her incredulous crew witnessed a miracle. Slowly at first and then with a great heave she lifted her head to the upward drag of the sail, and spilled half her load over the stern. Her gunwales came clear and she began to move, sluggish and waterlogged, but running again. Somebody caught up the drink keg and stove the head of it and bailed mightily with that. Among the haaf-men's strange mixture of sincere religious conviction and superstition, they had a strong belief that whatever evil agency sent you a sea like that one, if you survived it God in His mercy would grant you a respite to clear your boat before another boarding water came. So it was this time. No other big sea came over, and the boat's buoyancy increased by the minute as they flung the water out. Soon she was flying for the land once more, and her crew had a tale which the grandson of one told to me eighty or ninety years later. I had better add my personal conviction that this story is true. The incident was famous at the time and is still well remembered in Eshaness. It only remains to point out the obvious: that only a boat of the most perfect balance could have kept her keel under such circumstances, and only a skipper of iron nerve and first-class skill would have got her going.

THE GREAT DISASTER OF JULY, 1832

(*Shetland Life*. No. 25: November 1982)

There had been nothing to distinguish the early summer of 1832 from many another summer season in Shetland. Weatherwise, it had been disappointing. There had been odd fine days but from May onwards the wind had been too persistently out of the north, keeping the air cold and making folk complain: "Dis is shürely a year we're gjaun ta hae nae richt summer." We have heard such complaints more recently than 1832.

Yet on the whole, apart from the absence of sunny summer weather and though the growth of crops had been slow, the season had been moderate. There had been no violent interruptions to the haaf-fishing. Discomfort the fishermen had known as usual and there had been few enough days sufficiently warm to melt the tar inside a boat's gunwale; but discomfort was the haaf-man's inescapable portion at best of times, to be accepted and borne philosophically. Most fishermen had been more concerned during the early summer of 1832 that catches had been lighter than average.

Cholera was rife that year in the ports of Northern Europe and even in some of the ports and harbours of Britain, and there was great fear of the dreadful disease reaching Shetland. Most cosmopolitan of little ports, Lerwick attracted shipping from so many different quarters – and not least from the Baltic and Archangel – it seemed close to inevitable that sooner or later some vessel would bring the seeds of the foul plague here. A close watch was being kept, therefore, on all new arrivals.

Thus when the local packet schooner *Magnus Troil* came in from Leith on 11th July with a sick man on board she was unceremoniously hustled, passengers and all, to a quarantine berth in the North Harbour, there to await developments. And there she was to ride forlornly for many weary days with her passengers in a state of incipient mutiny and H.M. Revenue Cutter *Swan* as a watch-dog to prevent any communication with the shore.

The sick man died and was given a sea-burial from the schooner where she lay but whether his trouble was cholera is debatable. It is doubtful if anyone on board the *Troil* had ever seen the disease to recognise it for what it was, and failing expert medical diagnosis, it could have been anything. Certainly no other person was infected. But the *Magnus Troil* and her crew and passengers had to serve out a further term of quarantine until all risk of infection was finally removed. Among the quarantined passengers was a man who kept a journal. Edward Charleton was a young Englishman on a sight-seeing tour of Shetland. He had an eye for detail and his jottings are valuable.

At dawn on a quiet summer morning Bressay Sound provides as pleasing a prospect as you may find in any harbour in the kingdom and so it was on July 16th, 1832, a morning that gave no hint that that baleful date was to be graven for evermore on Shetland folk-memory. The *Magnus Troil* and her watch-dog, the *Swan* cutter sat on their own shadows, every rope and spar and the bends of their hulls reflected in the water below. There was no other vessel of any size in the harbour.

It has been said that even as the day spent there were no signs of impending ill weather. This is not merely incredible – the statement is untrue. Along the whole west side of Shetland a very heavy swell began setting in, great rollers coming out of the N.N.W. On the east side a curious phenomenon was noticed. The water was suddenly swarming with piltocks [coalfish] – so necessary for bait – while on the west not a tail was to be had out of the sea. There were other pointers, trifling some of them, but all assuredly noted and assessed by the weather-wise haaf-men.

On the other side of the coin there is a curious factor to be borne in mind here. Of all the months of the year July is the one month when the sky does not read true. The old men said: "Never heed a July sky". And it is true that the cloud formation called in Shetland a "wadder-heid" will stand from the western to the eastern horizon clear across the zenith for a whole day in July and nothing worse will materialise than a shower of rain. At any other season of the year a far less clear manifestation of that particular weather sign will send men looking to their boats and skroos [cornstacks] before dark for it is a sure sign of storm.

But signs and portents notwithstanding, if a haaf-skipper hoped to make a winning he did not flee at the first puff of wind. All up and down the east side of Shetland the sixerns were at sea. Only at Fethaland – where sixty boats were fishing – were they more cautious than usual. The Fethaland men contented themselves with only one set of lines that day and were back ashore by the first of the dark.

At North Yell a circumstance which had been regarded as a nuisance saved the fleet. All the sixerns there with one single exception had expended their bait on Monday and had come in too late to do anything about it that night. Consequently on Tuesday morning they had taken in their bait nets and were lying on the herring grounds close inshore when the weather changed. The exception was a sixern belonging to Thomas Irvine of Midbrake. She had indeed gone fram [offshore] but her skipper was careful and made the land safely with the first of the blow.

The sky in the N.N.W. had thickened over as the day spent but the wind had increased very little. About ten o'clock in the evening two Dutch busses came stealing into the harbour on the light breeze and brought up opposite the town. Taking along the Quarantine Doctor and the Dutch Vice-Consul, Customs House officers immediately boarded both vessels to seal up their bonded stores.

As everybody knew – and none better than the Customs man themselves – this sealing up was a mere hollow gesture. True, once in place, the seals would not be broken; but here and there stowed craftily in the big busses' capacious interiors, hidden in places that a month of rummaging would not reveal, would be enough *krooks* [stoneware bottles] of gin and big blue-paper packages of Dutch *hurl* [tobacco] to provide a very healthy little smuggle indeed when Dutchie judged the time was ripe. For such were the ways of the broad-beamed men from Enckhuizen and Vlaardigen – and nobody thought a whit the worse of them for it.

When the shore-party were ready to cross to the second buss the whole north sky had blackened over and it seemed that a heavy shower was setting up. The wind had also freshened and had suddenly become unbelievably cold. "As cauld as da breath o death itsel" said somebody; and maybe that was no bad description of what was abroad in the air that night. Hurrying, trying to beat the coming squall, almost on the stroke of midnight the Customs boat ran alongside the little stone jetty and the bowman jumped out to make the painter fast; and in the very same instant the threatening squall burst upon them in full and awful fury. No mere rain squall, this one, it was a full scale hail-storm, so that in seconds the boat's bottom was full of the stuff, stinging naked skin like the lash of a whip and making mens' feet to slip on the causey [cobbles] of the pier as they strove to snug their boat to safety.

In that first few hectic moments was established the pattern of what was to follow through the succeeding nights and days. Against a background of screaming tempest, unrelenting, never easing, were flung in fast succession those icy hail-squalls so that some men said later they bailed nearly as much hail as salt water. Was it surprising that so many died? Rather was it a matter for wonder that open boats could survive such conditions and live through even the first fearful night.

No lights were extinguished in Lerwick all night through. Along the foreshore blazing torches flickered and flamed and fought the gale and men hung about every sheltered corner. Lerwick waterfront was not lit at all then and bitter hard would it be to come safely in from the fury outside and be lost on the very doorstep of home. Sometime in the early morning a well-manned boat boarded the Revenue Cutter with a request from the local Commissioners of Supply that she put to sea to look for survivors. Somewhat reluctantly her Commander agreed and she got under weigh [raised anchor] shortly after daylight. But a similar request to the skippers of the two Dutch busses, Jakob van der Valk and his son Dirck, met with a flat refusal. There were already plenty of Dutch vessels in the vicinity, said the two, and they saw no sufficient reason why they should leave the sheltered harbour.

Morning came laggardly. After daylight one or two hardy souls on the *Troil* stuck their heads up to survey as scene such as they had never seen before but which would undoubtedly remain engraved on memory's eye as long as life lasted. The whole harbour seemed literally blown flat, a wilderness of snowy foam and fury. Great clouds of spindrift lifted till all the tortured sea seemed to be smoking together; and ever and again those villainous squalls came screaming and for a while the storm attained a crescendo almost beyond the compass of the human brain.

The schooner lay well enough. With her best and second bowers well home and her cables out to the clinch [bitter end], though she surged and shuddered to the savage jerking she was unlikely to move far. Down to leeward the two Dutch busses, having far less grip of the water than the heavy packet schooner, tumbled and danced like net-corks in a mill kloos. But they also were holding well.

Gazing to windward, the schooner's lads knew horror and despair; for they were Shetlanders too, knowing the score as well as anybody, and it must have truly seemed that no open boat, fashioned by the hand of man, could possibly survive in the horror they saw around them; and there were hundreds of their countrymen out there, missing and unaccounted for...

It was just then they sighted a sixern. They saw her sail first, a little smudge in the middle of the North Mouth, dark against the whiteness of a pursuing squall. For long minutes the squall hid everything and they thought the boat had gone. But as the smother cleared they saw her again, much nearer now. Again a squall overtook her and the towsman eased the halliards to let the boat drop behind the fury of it.

And now the watchers could see the sixern clearly. She was carrying her bow high, her stern well down, in splendid running trim, and they thought she must have fish on board for she seemed uncommonly deep. Only four men were visible: the skipper at the helm and the towsman at the tows, two others plying scoops in the owse-room when the tail of a sea came over – the exact number to sail the boat efficiently under such conditions and any more would be redundant.

Seeking the whereabouts of the two remaining men of the crew, it suddenly dawned on the *Troil's* men why the sixern was so deep. Sitting flat on the tulfirs in her bottom, their legs crossing in the middle of the boat, were not two men but *eight*. Somewhere in the holocaust out by, sometime during that fearful night and despite their own travail, that good skipper and his crew had contrived to snatch another full crew of fellow fishermen from the very jaws of death. Shame it is that nobody recorded that skipper's name. It was with admiration and deep respect for gallant seamen that they watched the boat kick defiant heels on the last mile of her journey until she vanished into safety at Freefield.

So Wednesday passed and another night, Thursday and Thursday night, and still the gale blew. All day on Friday it had moderated not one iota. Until at last on Saturday evening the weather broke. By dusk that night the wind was a gentle breeze and the thing was over. At least, the gale was over: the reckoning was yet to come.

In all the long chequered history of the Shetland fishing nobody had ever known of a storm like it. There had been summer gales in the past, some of them ferocious enough to cause death and suffering. The July gale of 1791 had been the cause of bringing in larger sixerns. But whether fierce and death-dealing or whether less fatal in their effects almost all of the summer gales known in Shetland had one thing in common: they were of short duration. The worst was generally over within the span of 24 hours.

Only the storm of '32 forgot to play to the rules and there is no doubt that this aberration contributed to the death toll. Basing their knowledge on previous experience, men believed even on the Friday morning that the weather must be on the point of breaking, We know that they were wrong and for all too many that final 24 hours was the final straw.

Not merely was this a matter of economic consideration, though very often boat and gear were all the material possessions a crew could call their own. There was something much deeper than that – a deep-seated affection of a man for his boat, for the well-trimmed little fabric which he had tested so often and so sorely and which had always proved true. When the cards were down for the final hand a man did not willingly fail his boat which had never failed him. On the second day of the gale Dutch skippers reported sadly that they had offered to relieve crews who would not leave their boats.

It has been stated glibly for the past 159 years that 105 fishermen lost their lives in 1832 and seventeen sixerns were lost. The first figure is unquestionably correct; the second is entirely misleading. The figure of seventeen boats merely records those craft lost with all hands, the fate of many which was known only to God and their dead crews.

These and their places of origin are listed as follows: from the island of Unst – five boats; from the island of Fetlar – one boat; from Mid and South Yell – five boats; from the parish of Nesting (and please note that this includes the island of Whalsay) – seven boats. Now I am perfectly aware that this, the official list, totals eighteen and not seventeen boats and the discrepancy of one I cannot explain. It may be that the Whalsay sixern, of which more later, was originally included and was not removed from the list when it became clear that she was not among those posted missing. The point is that the foregoing list takes no account of the numberless boats lost at sea but whose crews were saved.

The only bright spot in the whole affair and the factor which alone hindered the tragedy from being twice as terrible was the willing and eager help given by the Dutchmen, skippers and crews of the many herring busses on the coast. Those old-fashioned craft may have looked clumsy, even a little lubberly, yet sea-kindliness and the ability to accept with equanimity the worst that the North Sea had to fling about had been designed into their hulls long before by men who both built ships and sailed them. I doubt if their crews enjoyed the '32 gale any better than the other folk but at least they were better equipped than most to stand it.

From the very first morning after the storm broke busses were bringing in boats' crews. Skipper Hendrik van Rossen saved George Gilbertson and his crew from Whalsay. Skipper Hendrik Manneke brought in two crews – John Smith of Cunningsburgh and Garth Petrie from East Yell with all their men. On Sunday, 22nd July, Skipper Jacob Don turned up with Magnus Leask of Bressay and his men. Skipper Peter Roest, later the same day, came in with Robert Rendall of Burravoe and his crew and a second full crew whose identity are unknown. Skipper Arij van Roojan also brought in two crews – some of those survivors were from Lunnasting. Skipper Maartje de Heer saved another crew and Skipper Hermanus Kuiper of Emden brought in Robert Smith of Aith, Bressay and his crew. And the cutter *Swan* saved a crew of men. She returned from her requested cruise on Thursday bringing with her William Manson and his crew from Bressay.

Of all the short periods of Shetland history that I have researched in depth, over more than half a century, I know of no other time of tragedy that can even begin to parallel the five days of the storm of 1832 and the events that followed during ensuing weeks. The situation on shore was incredibly involved, a kaleidoscope of hope and utter despair which veered and changed from hour to hour. During the first two days of the tempest few of those who knew the conditions believed that more than a handful of men could have survived, assisted or unassisted, in the open sea. An awful mood of dull acceptance took over, that here at last was the catastrophe that spelled the annihilation of a whole generation of fishermen and the end of Shetland's haaf fishing for many a day to come.

Then as another day came up with the storm still roaring the Dutchmen began to bring in their quotas of living men, bloody indeed but still unbowed. Hope instantly fled to the zenith. These men who had survived three nights at sea were all good men but so were "wir" men – as good seamen and every bit as strong. If one crew could live through such nights so could others. Hope was abroad once more.

And indeed after that weekend when the sea smoothed and men's strength came back, scattered sixerns began to come in from southward in such numbers that it began to seem as though the dreaded butcher's bill might not be as heavy as had been feared. Nor was it. The total toll has been given as 105 men, the cream of Shetland's haaf fishermen, a shattering blow to a small community. But the numbers could have so easily been doubled.

Two different sources state categorically that no North Isles sixern fetched the land north of the Bard of Bressay. But from that point southward, to Sumburgh Head and beyond, they had found refuge on many ayres. Fladdabister, Cunningsburgh, Sandsaire, Levenwick, Troswick and Grutness

– they all had their quota and three separate sixerns made Fair Isle. One of these – or her crew – gave rise to much comment at the time. It appears that her skipper was an ancient mariner well-stricken in years who should have given up the haaf-man's tough calling long before. His crew were five boys in their 'teens. This rather unlikely little group survived the whole gale at sea when so many stronger men perished. They saw the storm blow itself out right to thr bitter end and proudly brought their boat into the South Harbour at the Fair Isle on the Sunday evening after the wind had broken with everybody still alive and still on the thwarts.

For many weeks after the disaster Shetland was rife with rumours of men being rescued by passing ships, of fishermen who had been carried far away to Aberdeen or Newcastle, to Antwerp and Norway and even across the Western Ocean. Poor folk, they were clutching at straws, still unwilling to accept the bitter terrible truth that their fathers, husbands, sons and brothers had gone for ever.

One such rumour, entirely incredible and quite untrue, has persisted to this day. On the second day of the gale the schooner *Norna,* contemporary and arch-rival of the *Magnus Troil* was lying hove-to on her passage from Leith to Lerwick. Bursting out of the smother to windward came an American barque scudding before the storm. As she passed close by the *Norna* the American hailed that she had on board fishermen whom she had just rescued.

That hurried hail was almost certainly misinterpreted. The *Norna's* man believed the American skipper to say that he had on board five crews. What he probably did say was that he had saved five fisherman. This would be the Whalsay crew picked up by the Boston barque of whom one man was drowned while boarding. A little more will be said about that later.

Naturally there was eager speculation as to when those five crews of men – thirty in all – would return to Shetland. Weeks passed and then months and hope was replaced with foreboding. What had the Americans done with them? Soon some foolish person revived an ancient yarn and suggested they had been carried to the Carolinas and Virginia and sold as plantation slaves.

This theory is of course quite fantastic. That free born British subjects, English speaking, could have been disposed of in this way in the southern states of America in the Year of Grace 1832 is not even worth discussion, This could have happened a century earlier – and there is even some evidence of such incidents – most surely not in the fourth decade of the nineteenth century. Yet the old story has persisted and has often been retold.

A fund on behalf of the destitute dependents was immediately started in London and raised the rather incredible sum – for a cause of this type and for an area so remote – of £3,086 18s 6d. Needless to say Arthur Anderson was behind the subscription list and served as treasurer to the committee.

Meanwhile in Shetland the Commissioners of Supply decided to make an award to the Dutch rescuers of five guineas for each individual crew saved. At the meeting in question some very complimentary things were said regarding the humanity and kindness of the Dutch skippers to fellow seafarers in distress. Among the incidents mentioned was the case of James Robertson of Lerwick, who had been snatched off the keel of a sixern by Skipper Jan van Duren of Zurikzee. He was the only man left alive of that vessel's crew. Gradually as the year progressed, far-fetched hopes faded. Widows, orphans and aged parents had to come to terms as best they could with the fact that there was nobody now to stand between them and the weather. Out of the broken fabric of their lives they now had to gather together an acceptable formula with which to start again. However hard it might be life had to go on. Then early in January 1833 there occurred an incident in Whalsay which came like a gleam of warm sunshine through the gloom.

Mention has been made already of a lost Whalsay sixern, five of whose crew were rescued by a passing American barque. This vessel was bound from the Baltic to Philadelphia. Kindly treated by the American crew, the Whalsay men were carried all the way across, landed in Philadelphia and put in care of the British Consul there.

Even with the best will in the world it took time to find a passage back to Britain and so it was only on the morning of 5th January 1833 – Auld Christmas Day – that they reached Lerwick on board the local sloop, *George Canning*. The day was windy and unpleasant and folk here urged the castaways to stay over one more night and get a better day on the morrow. But the Whalsay lads, not unnaturally, were in no mood for any more delay. A sixern was launched and ballasted and with a double reef tied the party set off for home. Although there was no way that news of their return could have reached the isle there was a large crowd waiting on the beach to meet them. The crowd, it is said, had been attracted by the strange behaviour of a dog belonging to one of the five men. After spending six months looking in vain for its master, it had gone down to the beach that morning and had spent several hours running along the shore, barking all the time and continually looking south towards Lerwick.

And so the account of the 1832 disaster was closed with one small entry on the credit side. There were other disasters to come, notably that of 1881 whose centenary was so ably commemorated last year, but the disaster of 1832 even at this distance in time still looms on the horizon as the greatest single tragedy in the history of our islands.

THE HALF-DECKERS

A Story of Success and Failure

(*Shetland Folk Book*. Volume VII: 1980)

Herring fishing as an organised industry in Shetland, unlike the haaf or white fishing, does not have a history dating back to remote antiquity. It is true that for centuries, when herring shoals set into the voes as they were wont to do most summers, a few hundred barrels would be caught and cured. But prior to the beginning of the 19th century, apart from various grandiose and subsidised British schemes which all ended in failure, the great herring stocks of the Shetland seas were left almost entirely to the Dutch.

Some of the causes of British failure in these enterprises may be attributed to mismanagement and lack of practical knowledge by the promoters. Fishing craft were large – in fact, even under the bounty scheme of 1808 eligible vessels had to be between 60 and 100 tons to qualify. Herrings were gutted, salted and packed on board, entailing an enormous crew which obviously must include all the fish-workers and coopers necessary for the complete process of cure. This was a carbon copy of the methods which the Dutch had used for centuries, but the crews of the British busses seemed to lack the expertise and skill of the canny Hollanders.

The fundamental fault did not lie with the crews. It apparently never occurred to anybody connected with these schemes that a method which was the only one possible for foreign fishermen working far from home off a strange and sometimes hostile coast, was cumbersome, unwieldy and entirely unnecessary when operated by British fishermen seldom more than twenty miles from their native shore. The answer lay in a shore-based curing station and a smaller fishing craft which could be handled easily by half a dozen men, the minimum number required to shoot and hail her nets.

This shore-based technique was first adopted along the coast of the Scottish mainland and had become general by the second decade of the nineteenth century. On both sides of the Forth, at Peterhead, at all the small Moray Firth ports, and especially at Wick, herring curing was well established and the fleets of herring luggers were increasing year by year. Even in Orkney by the end of that decade the herring fishing was already of considerable economic importance. Only in Shetland, better situated as a herring centre than any of these places, was the business still neglected.

Not until 1819 was a syndicate formed at Lerwick for the express purpose of establishing a Shetland herring fishery. Members of this group; the

The Shetland herring "half-decker" *Favourite* shows the typical gaff rig adopted in place of the traditional Shetland squaresail and the "half-deck" layout. Model by John Shewan for Royal Scottish Museums, 1952.

Zetland Herring Fishing Coy., were local business men and fish curers, but their secretary and the driving force behind the whole enterprise was Andrew Duncan, Sheriff Substitute of Shetland. Without his enthusiasm and initiative it is doubtful if the scheme would have ever got off the ground.

Through the helpful agency of Samual Laing of Papdale, orders were placed with an Orkney boatbuilder for two boats, complete and ready to run the fishing, of the model and type being used by the Orkney fishermen. The boats were delivered in the spring of 1821, the very first two purpose-built herring boats ever owned in Shetland. It is worth recording their names. They were, rather appositely, the *Experiment* and the *Hope*, of 26 feet and 23 feet keel length respectively. And, a significant sidelight on how novel this type of fishing was in Shetland, two experienced skippers for the new boats, Thomas Carens and James Patrick, were engaged from the town of Leven in Fife, because "Our fishermen knows almost nothing about how the operations of the Fishery are performed, notwithstanding their frequent intercourse with the Dutch".

The start of the new venture was anything but promising: in fact, the first season's fishing was almost a total failure and the second not much better. But after that things began to improve and suddenly more boats were acquired by Shetland owners. Five years after the shaky start the fishing could be said to be truly under way. Then came a bumper season in 1826 when practically every boat engaged made a "winning" and from that point the new industry never looked back. The beginning of the 1830s saw it assume the proportions of a modest boom with boats being acquired and built by the score.

Various writers have tried to account for this sudden popularity of an industry which had been so long neglected. A favourite theory has been that following the fishing disaster of 1832 when seventeen sixerns and over a hundred men were lost, Shetland fishermen lost confidence in the open haaf boat. This may have been a contributory factor but it was not the only cause. The sixern and the haaf fishing flourished for many a long year after 1832. There were other reasons. It must not be overlooked that the rise of the herring fishing corresponded with the failure of the cod fishery on the Regent Bank, that Golconda to westward of Foula which a few years previously had been described as inexhaustible. In 1833 the so-called home-codfishing was such an utter failure that Hay & Ogilvy sent three of their sloops to fish on the Faroe Bank, the first beginning of the Shetland/Faroe fishing. This corresponded in 1834 with a record herring season when 41,000 barrels were cured. And there was yet another potent reason. To induce men to take up the herring fishing, owners of boats had introduced a more open and generous system of settlement with their share-fishermen than the haaf-men had ever known. A man's earnings might be small, at least he got what was due to him in cash when the herring season was done. Many crews managed to save enough to buy shares in their boats and even in some cases to buy their boats outright. There was hope in the future, a degree of prosperity not known for generations, and it is one of the saddest tragedies of the time on the islands that all was doomed to failure in the end.

Compulsory registration of fishing boats had not begun at this period and what statistics there are lump herring boats and sixerns together. It is thus impossible to compute with any accuracy the number of true herring boats owned in Shetland at the peak of the fishing. A writer of the 19th century has put the number at "upwards of 300" and this is almost certainly an understatement. Hay & Ogilvy, the principal firm then engaged, owned in the region of one hundred themselves.

When Ployen reviewed this fleet in the course of his famous "Voyage" in 1839, he saw a heterogeneous collection of models and rigs which bewildered the poor man. There were one- and two-masted luggers from Wick and the Moray Firth; more shapely steep-sterned luggers from the Firth of Forth: big South Isles yoles from Orkney setting two spritsails instead of lugs. With his inquisitive bent for working out logical reasons for all that was new to him, Ployen could only conclude that that the industry being only a scant twenty years old, Shetland fishermen had not yet made up their minds which type of boat was best suited to the fishing.

A facile conclusion but an erroneous one. What the good Dane did not realise was the fact that many of the boats had been purchased from elsewhere by men whose means were too slight to allow them freedom of choice. The weird mixture of hulls and rigs merely represented individual boat fashions in the areas from which they had come. A little local guidance could have convinced him that the Shetland fishermen had indeed made up their minds and a local herring boat was emerging sufficiently distinctive to warrant a descriptive term which survives to this day. This was the "half-decker," a craft not so very different from others along the coasts of Northern Scotland, yet in certain respects very peculiarly Shetland's own.

By the late 1830's a substantial portion of the herring fleet had been built for Shetland owners. Many had been built locally, notably at Hay & Ogilvy's yard at Freefield, but also at Sandsair, Cunningsburgh, Scalloway and Unst. Others had been ordered from yards outwith Shetland, especially from Wick and Orkney.

Measuring between 30' and 33' in keel length, the Shetland half-decked herring boat favoured the Fife rather than Moray Firth hull. Clinker-built, she was fairly beamy but sharp enough in the bottom to make her reasonably stiff under sail. Her forefoot was rounded to a graceful curve which began as high as the bobstay shackle and her sharp stern was perpendicular with, of course, the rudder hung outside. Inboard she was entirely open save for a sharp forecastle deck from the mast to the stem, under which a spartan meal could be cooked over a fire-kettle and where it was possible for her crew to snatch an hour or two of uncomfortable sleep.

The greatest difference between this boat and craft from the Scots ports lay less in her hull than in her rig. For a reason which is obscure, Shetland fishermen never favoured the lug sail though the Scots shifting lug is far closer to the traditional Shetland squaresail than is a gaff mainsail. Yet the latter was universally used in the islands from the beginning to the very end of the Shatland sailing drift-net herring boat. So the half-decker, like her larger successor, set gaff mainsail, stay foresail and jib. When a lug sail was used it was generally a standing lug with the tack to the mast rather than to the stem.

Each boat carried a crew of six men and a fleet of not more than twenty-five nets which had to be shot and hailed by hand. There were no mechanical aids. The nets were made of hemp twine, rather stiff and incredibly strong. It was said that if a button on a man's clothing caught when shooting, the button either tore out or the man went overboard. The mesh did not break. As a preservation the nets were immersed in a boiling solution of birch-bark at regular intervals during the fishing.

No bush-rope was used. Instead, above the corks along the head-line each net was furnished with a strong rope balk which took the strain when hailing, while along the bottom were stone weights to keep the net perpendicular in the water. Each net was attached at its four corners to its neighbours on either side with a buoy between each two, and when a boat was "shot aff" – that is, when her nets were all set – she rode to the fleet by a heavy warp called the swing. It was not unknown for a boat to lose all her gear through the swing breaking on a rough night. After the nets were set the rudder was generally unshipped and taken inboard, often giving the crew a nasty job in the morning to get the thing back in place before making sail.

Buoys – or bows – were of sheepskin, calfskin, sometimes of dogskin, with a painted wooden keg at the tail, half, and quarter marks.

A few names of those boats turn up in old accounts: *Erne, Argo, Falcon, Eagle, Struggler, Pirate, Rob Roy, Garland* – ordinary and common-place enough. The biggest boat in the fleet in 1840 was the *Mariner* of Lerwick, 36' of keel and fully decked. (I cannot resist adding that she was skippered by William Henderson of Southerhouse, South Scousburgh, my great-grandfather). That this boat represented the next stage of further development there can be little doubt. Had the fishing continued there would soon have been more boats like the *Mariner*. But it was not to be. Nemesis, unseen and unsuspected, was coming close.

All fishing is a game of chance and herring fishing more than most. And perhaps it is this very fact which constitutes its greatest fascination for men over the year, its appeal to the gambler latent in most of us. It is the anticipation, the thrill of the fat cow turning up when other kine are lean and bony, that has kept some men in thrall to the herring fishing even when more prosaic work with assured returns beckoned.

So when the fishing fell away after the record season of 1834 the industry carried on, fishermen, curers and financiers alike waiting for the better times which must be just around the corner. But the returns for the next few years were not encouraging. In 1835 herrings cured in Shetland totalled 32,192 barrels; in 1836 the catch was down by nearly 10,000 to 22,500 barrels; and in the following year only 17,684 barrels were cured. The season of 1838 showed a slight improvement with 19,270 barrels, and then in 1839 came the poorest catch for many years with only 16,522 barrels packed. Curers and fisherman alike were feeling the draught and the boat-owners most committed to the fishing more than any.

Behind the whole fishing industry of Shetland, by this time carrying credits for all, was the Shetland Bank, so inextricably linked with the whole complex operation that it was often referred to as the Fishermen's Bank. Not surprisingly, by 1840 the bank was feeling the strain of three successive poor seasons coupled to the fact that the white-fishing over the same period had not produced the returns of former years. Nor should it be overlooked that the principals of this local financial concern were Messrs. Hay & Ogilvy, the largest commercial house in Shetland with wide interests, but whose main business was boat-owning, fishing, and fish-curing.

Despite the poor returns of recent years, the late fishing of 1840 began in some spirit of optimism. Catches during August had been light but regular. There was herring on the grounds and it was hoped that during September fishermen would make up their leeway. Instead, on the night of Tuesday, 9th September, 1840, there burst on the fleet "the most severe gale of wind known in the memory of the oldest in Shetland at this season of the year".

There had been enough signs of the coming gale to make skippers uneasy. Some had remained in port and others had borne up for harbour again without setting a net. But by far the greater part of the fleet were at sea, mainly south and east of Sumburgh Head, and when the storm fell on them like the wrath of God out of a black September night it caught most of these riding to their nets.

It has been said that not a net that was in the water that night was ever hailed [hauled]. Most boats cut away at once and, with the last reef-point tied, made for the land. Others tried to ride it out, hanging on to their gear until the swings parted, by which time the wind was too fierce to carry sail at all. Details of what happened to a few of these will be told later. Here it will serve to say merely that the loss was staggering. Five boats went with all hands that night, and over thirty men lost their lives. Though a great many crews made the land, even there they found no safety. In Lerwick there was utter chaos, boats dragging and driving everywhere, many being smashed to pieces on the shore. There were similar scenes at Scalloway and elsewhere. Thirty boats were totally lost and scores of others were damaged, many beyond repair.

Coming after the years of recession, this was a disaster of the first magnitude for the Shetland herring fishery. The local Fishery Officer, writing immediately after the gale, describes "the loss of Lines, Boats, Nets and other materials as being of an extent beyond my computation..." Nor did he exaggerate. So great was the damage that the whole industry was paralysed. Repair and replacement of boats alone would take time and much material, and even with the boats ready for sea there was not in Shetland a fraction of the nets and gear needed to rig out the fleet once more. The cost of all this in comparative terms and in relation to the community concerned came to an enormous sum – and the whole return for that disastrous fishing season amounted to only 4,397 barrels of cured herring.

Things lagged over the winter. Money was tight, credit not obtainable. Moreover whispers were abroad that all was not well with the affairs of a concern which had been regarded for many years as being sound as the Bank of England. Many men who were wholly committed to the herring fishing faced the new season with foreboding and near despair.

Haaf-fishing, mainstay of the Shetland economy, must go on and the sixerns rigged out as usual in 1841. Not so the herring boats. Only a very few were in trim for the late fishing. An unverified note puts the number at sixty, which is probably correct. It was a great pity that this should have been so for herrings were much more plentiful than for several years. Even this travesty of a fishing fleet, augmented by the sixerns' efforts after Lammas [1st August], brought 14,337 barrels to cure.

The same spirit of uncertainty ushered in the season af 1842. Fishing is a game of chance at best and those who follow the trade are accustomed to riding out the poor and scanty season, confident that a better year will come. But the present situation went beyond all that. Younger men began to drift away in scores to the Merchant Service: to Greenock and Glasgow to sign-on for the Quebec timber trade, to Liverpool and London to ship for Australia and the Far East. Rumours were more rife than ever, until suddenly these hardened into fact and there fell the most shattering blow of all: the firm of Hay & Ogilvy signed a trust deed and the Shetland Bank closed its doors with liabilities in excess of £60,000.

The failure was no reflection on the business acumen of partners in an honourable and respected firm, nor was it brought about by recklessness or mismanagement. These were parlous times on the world of commerce. The immediate cause of the crash was certainly the strain imposed by the fishing disaster and its aftermath, but there were other factors also in a wider context. The abolition of bounties on cured fish in 1829/30 was one; of far graver import was the depression of the West Indies and Irish markets for cured fish, due in the one case to the emancipation of the slaves and in the other to the wretched, poverty-stricken state of the country. All of this bore hard on a firm whose main assets were all tied up in fishing and sea-borne trade.

Whatever the reasons, the bank crash fell on the economies of Shetland as the gale had burst on the fishing fleet and with much the same result. Writing to the Honourable Board of Customs in Edinburgh in 1843, a local Customs Officer regrets that he has almost nothing to report: "The whole trade of this country has been laid prostrate by the failure of this one commercial house..." The Fishery Officer strikes an even more despondent note: "...the commercial distress... from which Shetland has not been excepted, has reduced it to a very low ebb, many being of the opinion that it has not been in such a state for at least fifty years".

Life must go on and men must strive for a living, whether by land or sea. In mid-19th century Shetland there was no option: the living must come from the ocean in one way or another. So out of the debris of 1842 the fishing industry rose again, the haaf-fishing and the "home" cod-fishing. Shetland vessels began to range far afield seeking the cod, big schooners like the *Janet Hay* to Davis Straits, other schooners and smacks to the Faroe Bank and the coast of Iceland. Gradually life came back to normal – though for fifty years afterwards folk still spoke of the "hungry Forties".

But for almost another forty years the herring industry was not revived. Boats which had been hauled ashore in 1840 were never launched again, were left to moulder and rot on their shores – as many writers have noted, though almost none have produced an accurate and logical reason why.

The reason why these events have been so consistently ignored by the chroniclers of 19th century Shetland is not easy to explain. While, as has been said, there have been many references to the collapse of the herring fishing, no contemporary writer has detailed the circumstances leading up to that catastrophe. In recent years both Hance Smith and J.R. Nicolson have outlined the true facts, but in his none-too-accurate "Sail Fishermen of Shetland" Halcrow is inexcusably misleading. He states categorically that "... there were no great disasters" while at the same time he admits having heard mystifying tales of boats being driven off the land and men being rescued after many days at sea. The reason he gives for the failure of the fishing is positively ludicrous: that the landlord/merchant (his special *bête noire*) "whose main financial interests were in the half-decker," suddenly refused credit to their fishermen. These in turn "became defiant" and refused to go to sea. Surely, from the points of view of both owners and men, a classic example of cutting off noses to spite faces.

The account I have set down here may be verified by anyone who cares to do a little intelligent research in the records of the local Fishery Office and of Lerwick Custom House, and especially in the invaluable archives of Messrs. Hay & Co. – which archives include the letter-book of Sheriff-Substitute Andrew Duncan. Much may be gleaned also from contemporary newspapers: the "Scotsman," John O'Groats Journal" and the old "Aberdeen Herald".

What is even more puzzling then the absence of published records is the strange fact that almost every trace of the 1840 storm appears to have been erased from folk-memory in Shetland. In the field of Shetland folklore, where tales of sea adventure and disaster are so prominent a part, it is incomprehensible that memories of this one event with its far-reaching consequences seem to have slipped completely into obscurity.

It was not always so. As a lad growing up in Dunrossness I listened to many stories of "da gale when da herrin boats were lost." Some of those unforgotten yarns are related here, corroborated and enlarged from my father's notes and notebooks of my friend, the late R. Stewart Bruce.

The weather was moderate on that Tuesday, 9th September, 1840, and many weather-wise skippers, sensing trouble, doubted the wisdom of going off. In the event, however, while a few remained at anchor most of the fleet sailed though not all set their nets. But most of the boats were "shot aff" down to the south and east of Lerwick when the wind cameout of the N.N.W. about 9 p.m. Within an hour they were battling for their lives in the teeth of a hurricane. The night was as black as pitch, spindrift blinding, and boats groping for the land had little idea of where they were. All agreed that making landfall was the most hazardous part of all.

Whalsay men had read the signs right and were hesitating when William Budge, the Laird's factor, came down and, accusing them of faint-heartedness, ordered them to sea. As might be supposed, a major row developed. Eventually, the fishermen went but against their better judgement and most of them dodged in the lee of the land without shooting. These were soon in shelter, though not all made harbour safely. The *Erin,* skipper Thomas Anderson, was wrecked at the point of Tonga, the *Erne* at the West Hole of Gruid, and the *Falcon* at Snarra Geo, Sandwick. Another boat went to pieces on the Holm of Sandwick and her crew spent a miserable night on the holm before being rescued next day. James Tait of Houster, Tingwall, deliberately beached his boat on the sand at Symbister and saved both boat and crew.

Everywhere the same story was being repeated. The Lerwick boat *Struggler*, skipper Robert Henderson, after threshing safely up to the land, missed stays in the North Mouth coming into Lerwick and was smashed to pieces.

But the boats furthest down to southward suffered most. The laggard dawn of Wednesday morning came upon a terrifying scene; a shrieking tempest tearing the sea to madness, spindrift blinding vision to a few hundred yards so that each swamping boat was a forlorn entity whose despairing crew pumped and bailed for their lives in a travail of their own. For, do not forget, those little craft were but open boats at best.

There were tragedies enough, but the loss of life would have been far greater but for the fact that a singular number of larger vessels happened to be in the vicinity of Shetland that night. A Dutch lugger picked up one crew and carried them to Holland. Similarly, a Flemish fisherman took the men out of another boat and landed them at Nieuport, in Belgium, whence they were shipped across to Dover by the Ostend packet.

But most of the strange craft caught off Shetland by the storm were French fishing schooners, homeward bound after their season on the Iceland cod-banks. A Dunrossness crew in a foundering boat drove down on one of them lying hove-to. No sooner were they sighted than the Frenchman filled away on their ship, worked up to the herring boat and fielded the crew out of her very neatly. Not willing to let the boat go, she was swung astern of the schooner. Later on the Shetland skipper was wakened out of exhausted slumber by his rescuer.

"You come now," the Frenchman whispered, "your leetil bateau ees all forlorn." The boat was on the point of sinking and he wished her skipper to see her before she was cut away.

This schooner belonged to one of the Breton ports – St. Malo, Paimpol, Concarneau? – and the Shetland fishermen had a long and weary journey on foot to one of the north Channel ports from which they got a hitch across to England. It so happened that one of them had his small son off to the fishing with him on that fateful night. Tramping along the French coast, when the little boy's legs tired the older men took turns carrying him. This party related that they never wanted for food during all their long journey. At every town and fishing village along the coast kindly folk supplied their needs unasked.

Another Dunrossness crew were picked up by a schooner from Dunkirk. There was no finesse about this rescue. Working up to windward of the sinking boat as the Breton had done, a hail in good English warned the Shetland men to stand by. Down the big schooner came along the boat's weather side, lying down to the gale, her numerous crew lining her lee rail. As she crashed alongside the fishermen jumped for their lived and were dragged helter-skelter on board while their boat went astern with her whole weather side stove in.

This schooner had made a poor voyage and fished for a further spell on the Dogger Bank before returning to Dunkirk. It was thus many weeks before the shipwrecked fishermen got back to Shetland. On a grey winter morning Christie Gilbertson of Braemar opened the door of his home at last, to be confronted by his young wife clad in mourning black from top to toe.

Yet another Dunrossness crew owed their lives to a different sort of craft. This was the fine cutter yacht *Osprey*, owned by a Colonel Lumley, returning from a hunting trip in Northern Norway. One of the party on board was Frederick Dundas, M.P. for Orkney and Zetland. Like the Frenchman, the yacht was lying hove-to when the sinking boat was sighted. Superbly handled, she ratched [sailed slowly] close to windward while a lifebuoy attached to a lead-line was drifted down. By this means a warp was hauled across and made fast to the herring boat's mast, after which the cutter slipped to leeward and rode to the waterlogged boat as to a sea anchor, while her crew were dragged through the water, one at a time, by means of the lifebuoy and the line.

The *Osprey* landed her castaways at Aberdeen, eleven men in all, she having saved a second crew of whom I know nothing. On the same day a Scots brig bound for Hull touched along Aberdeen Bay to land yet another crew.

There is a pleasant sequel to the *Osprey* rescue. The Shetland men were greatly impressed by the kindness and fine seamanship of Captain William Payne, master of the yacht. When later on a son was born to the wife of Peter Goudie of Lunabister, one of the Shetland crew, the boy was christened William Payne Goudie after his father's rescuer.

The boat *Confidence* of Nesting, skipper Arthur White, ran before the gale and had made the coast of Norway somewhere near Bergen by the time the wind broke. Her exhausted men were desperate to land but White would have none of it and bore up for Shetland. They reached Lerwick on Sunday, 19th September, ten days from the time they had put to sea.

A Mossbank boat, Skipper Magnus Murray, also reached Norway and her crew got safely ashore in the sheltered head of a fjord. They were sent back to Hull by the British Consul and eventually came home to Shetland by the mail steamer *Sovereign* from Leith. Sadly, poor Murray's troubles were not over. He found that his wife, pregnant and near her time when he left her, had by anxiety and grief been prematurely brought to bed and both mother and baby had died.

Charles Johnson

Charles Johnson.
Photo courtesy Robert Johnson

Charles Johnson was born at Houlland, North Roe in 1861 and died at Toam, North Roe in 1938. He was one of a family of 12, and his father was one of the prominent haaf skippers of the era. His adult fishing career began in sixerns at the haaf, followed by spells in Faroe cod smacks and local herring boats. He gave up the sea and became a barman in the Grand Hotel in Lerwick for some years, before moving to Newcastle to join his brother Laurence who had a licensed trade business there. He returned to North Roe before the First World War, and settled down to crofting life. Charles's schooling – during the pre-School Board era – was in the Methodist School in North Roe, and he must have been a good scholar. For the fiftieth anniversary of the haaf fishing disaster of July 1881 he wrote an account of his experiences as a young man in a haaf sixern during the storm, and how she made safe landing in Ronas Voe after a hair-raising four-hour passage from 36 sea miles offshore.

This was published in Manson's Shetland Almanac of 1932, to great acclaim: here was the authentic voice of the haaf-man telling the tale from first-hand experience. He followed this with an account of his experiences in the storm of 1887 – better known as the 'Whalsay Disaster,' – and a stirring defence of the haaf fishery, also in Manson's almanac a year after his death in 1938. His writings are unique, for no other haaf-man put pen to paper, and his straightforward style and modest treatment of his own abilities only enhance the power of his narratives.

THE 1881 DISASTER

Experiences of a Northmavine survivor, told by Himself Fifty Years Later (Manson's Shetland Almanac. 1932)

We were fishing at Uyea, Northmavine. Our crew was seven – four older men and three youths – my first season as a man in a offshore boat. Three of the older men was our leading men. Us other four did not interfere at any time. The day referred to was a early morning start; they were astir at five to get a help from the west tide. We were one of three boats who pulled west and off till we got the Ossa through marks in the Heylor land. These land-marks with the compass led us out a N.W. Using eight oars we pulled nine hours in a smooth sea. We lost sight of the other two boats to the east'ard: it was hazy. This would take us off shore about thirty miles on the Ronasvoe fishing ground known to us as Heylor hills. We shutt our six lines N.W. by N., which would reach close on six miles and run down on 96 fathoms' water. We had a feed, which took less than an hour, and commenced to haul.

The tide runs mostly east, so we don't wait for a turn, and if there were fish there might be dogs. We got fish at once – very large ling. We hauled three lines to our mid-buoy and sinker (we did not lift that) and had got 180 ling with a scatter of other fish, which filled the boat's shott level with the toft. They say the weather is fine and nothing to show otherways. There is fish here; our hooked fish is not tampered with. We will shutt out these three wet lines a N.N.E. My job at shutting was to cut up fish for bait.

We had come well through with our first line when it came a bat of wind from N. with a little wet. I said to the men shouting "Is this a change?" they did not answer me. That passed away and the sea fell flat. Anyone could see it was a change, but no remarks were passed. These men were not careless about the weather: they would think, "It's as good to be shutting as doing anything else till the coarse weather comes." They did not know when it would come nor where it would come from. The idea was, when these three lines was shutt, we would run down, take time and clean up the fish we had got and put the none-market fish and the refuse that was of use in a place by itself, so as it could be thrown if need be. In hauling, again, we might get more than the boat could carry, and the none-market fish would be the first.

We had come a short way through our second line when we heard and saw the weather coming. It struck us about on the bow, and being heavy aft, of course she payed off: The sea commenced to rain over us. The two men stopped shutting; me and another youth took their place, and shifting places is take and give a chance to put on oilskins; we started to haul back. The skipper turned to a man who had been a skipper and asked him what he had to say about this. He replied, "Making for the land now we will come there in the darkness." These men was cool, and spoke the matter over. We had the two places, the South Wick, Uyea, and Ronasvoe; the next port Hamnavoe, Eshaness, or around Eshaness to the Minn. They decided to try back as we had come; which of the two places, the South Wick or Ronasvoe, was not mentioned; it appears that was left to the skipper. The weather being fine, we were working from the owse-room – a place reserved for bailing water, the mid-room being the working-room proper. We were thus not prepared for bailing, and the breakers was threatening us all around. We could not further manage the boat with oars, and could not haul lines. We were being blown out of that direction. We had come now to our fished lines, and lifted our mid-buoy and sinker; the fish then floated our lines to the surface: we saw the fish as far as we could see. Our men did not want any more fish: they were satisfied with the boat's weight and trim, so the lines were cut. We could not give the boat a fair chance without a bit of sail; when the lines was cut she was put before the wind and we prepared for bailing water. The skipper told us it was 9.30 p.m., and the wind was N. by E. When he was ready aft we put up the mast and she commenced her race. We close-reefed the sail, put the tack forat, and two men took the halyards. The sail was not meant for speed. It's to set to take her away from the seas, and they will be better able to manage her among the seas having the sail to set. We then bailed the water out; there was a sap in her, not a lot: she had only been taking small wash and sprays. We were lucky we got a chance to get under way and none of that seas to break over us. She goes away all right; she's foaming at the bows under the bare mast, and when she gets a bit of sail she's very sore pressed. To my thinking she's too deep in the water; she could not take more fish aft in any case; but I passed no remark, and to begin with they said the boat was in good trim.

The skipper, when we were getting under way, took notice of the wind by the compass – the wind had to be his guide. They did not expect the wind to shift after the first bat. There would be wild steering in any case when the water was going over the boat and flooding the glass of the compass, and no suitable place for it in front of the man steering. In still weather they were all right. In this case steering by a compass could not be done. She was not taking much water – just sprays and wash anof to keep the shovel going in the owse-room. I noticed he run the seas in their weakest parts, what we called the tails, sometimes the first tail, but he often got along to the last tail – so often, and being on an easterly tack, we four who had nothing to do with managing the boat thought we were getting east, as we had to get east, about five miles for the South Wick and a much shorter distance for Ronas Voe. Going back the opposite course to that we went would be fatal: we would come down on the Okern Heads. In fact, missing any of these two ports might be fatal.

Only once did I notice him having to run a sea in the centre. This sea rose very high astern. They pressed her with the sail when the surge came around her, and although the sail was laid down she run it for a bit (like a field of snow) and took water over both sides. It was not good to look at, but it was only a look. She could not have stood much of that. She took the water from the mast aft to the owes-room, so it came only in the mid- and owes-room, and was not a lot, but we were standing on the boddom to the boot-tops in the owes-room. The water could not get aft through the fish; the fish dammed it forat. The boat being heaviest aft, the water all came from forat to the owes-room, so for bailing the shovel could do. The three men who were managing the boat did not pass any remarks to us nor to one another; they appeared to be quite contented and fairly understood what they were doing. I had been brought up with boating since I was a child, but this of course was a bit extra.

It would have been from about 11p.m. till it might have been 12, that it was some darker, but not too dark: we could see our surroundings during this time. She took more water, not breaking seas. There was a heavy westerly japp [short steep seas] knocking up against her, not too bad, just what we usually called "lucky lumps," but with that and the sprays the shovel had to be kept going. The breaking seas kept on the same, no better. After what I thought was passing 12, it was more lighter – we could see much farther and thought we would see the low land first. These men did not say when we might see land or what land we might see first. The skipper, a man of good knowledge, perhaps never was trying for the South Wick, and thought it needless to do so (South Wick is to the westward of the Isle of Uyea). Us noticing how he was doing, and sometimes getting along a bit with almost a beam wind, we thought we were getting east, and expected to see the Isle first. It was getting lighter, and we could have seen land a good way off, so we looked on the water mostly ahead, and by and by we seen land and reported the Isle; it bore forat on the bow to leeward and he stood on it. To the east'ard of the Isle would be no use; but as luck would have it we seen at once that it was the Ossa, and told him. He came back as he was before with the wind; then he run a sea and came up with her until the wind was almost a-beam. This I did not understand, as we were in a fair way for Ronas Voe. Without any remarks being passed, I came to see that we told him it was the Isle, and now we tell him it's the Ossa – he's come up to try and make sure.

He had just well got up when a sea made, as usual in such cases. They gave her the sail, or more sail. He did not run that sea, it was too close on us;

he just kept her going; the last tail struck her from the mast and aft. She lay down to this – that's the sail. She had no high side to receive a big knock. It's the only time she's laying down to it since we started. She was submerged where the sea came; I lost sight of the man in the owes-room and the skipper, and as it passed over her he rather kept her away, and the sail was eased. There was a lot of water in the owes-room, and some in the mid-room where the men sat at the sail. The shott could not take water, it was full of fish. The hole of the shott where the skipper sat was full : it's a small place. The water from there settles down, runs under the fish and comes in the owes-room. We had a boddom-board, a little boom, and our mid-buoy on the top of the fish; it was washed off. We thought we did not lose any fish. We had a shifting-board that ships fore-and-aft the shott and forms a bulks-head; it was always shipped in when we started to haul lines. It is required and is safest in every case when there's fish in the shott, especially when tacking. In this case it would help to stop the water from disturbing the fish and getting underneath the top ones. They were big heavy ling lying fore-and-aft. When she was clear of this sea there was no water in her to be excited about: the shovel did it. I said this last sea was too close on us to be run, Yes – coming from a beam wind to nearly dead before, there's delay in that. In trying to run, the sea would break over the starn and go first over. Keeping her going there's a chance of getting clear. In this case we got clear to half the boat's length.

It's much lighter now and we have had no reason to complain of the darkness. It's not been all times alike, but never what we called darkness. The good man who mentioned the land and darkness did not mean that we were to stop where we were. His system was when in difficulty with his boat was, get under way. His statement meant a lot. Can the skipper face running on a lee shore? Will the idea not interfere with his work in managing the boat? If he could not face it then he meant to propose running to the westward, clear of the land. He did not expect the wind to last long. I was told by people ashore that the wind broke at 1 a.m., us at sea would not notice it. I for one was glad when the lines were cut and the boat got her freedom. Put her to do what's right and she will do it. It's no use putting her to do what's seen as too much till the last chance.

The last sea I have described appeared to be the last of the breaking seas. We got out of them and saw Ronasvoe more clear. It's high land, so we were still a good way off. There was a change in the sea, but very big rollers. I did not notice the wind any less. I went forat under the sail and had a look over the bows, and she was like running over a precipice; but it would settle away underneath her and another one rise in front. I seen we were clear of the breaking seas. I thought that odd, as we were not still in line with the Heads, and they had still to keep the sail low and ease as she fell forat over the sea. I felt relieved when I seen we were not likely to take any more water. Although we had no reason to complain, any water in a boat is enough. Our men said they were satisfied with the boats weight. What about taking 12 or 17 cwts. of water? Water in a boat is weight and worse than weight. I would like some people to understand what water in a boat means. These open boats had no bulksheads across them – having that would not work, I suppose. What they had was open grating between rooms or compartments, so that water could pass almost at will from aft to forat or vice-versa. Say a boat has an empty shott and she ships a sea and partly fills the shott and owes-room – she lifts well aft, it all seeks forat to the lee bow. Say this happens with the shott half full of fish – it's not so easy bailing water mixed with fish. Then every time the boat rolls the water rolls with her, so in a heavy sea, when up to the boot-tops at the knee, knowing that's in the owes-room and even with only a little in the mid-room, that was as much as I wanted to see, yet she would not be quarter-full.

The skipper kept on for the east side of Ronasvoe in case he might have to run a sea. The sea was very bad on both sides of the entrance; the west side was the worst: it's the most rocky side. When we got inside the Heads he drew into the centre of the entrance and headed on towards the Blade of Heylor. We seen there was a lot of boats there; we came in-about and tied up; we got out; the skipper having a watch told us it was 1.30 a.m. – four hours running in. We were nothing the worse; we had not been afloat twenty-four hours, we had not completed a night's none-rest. True, we had pulled offshore the day before, but in our line that was just an ordinary day's work. About the distances offshore, all that I am sure about is the time. I would think she made over seven miles an hour of a streight course; I have not thought she made eight. She had no stoppage, only wild steering and foaming almost all the time, and sometimes too sorely pressed. So any of my readers who knows about a boat of this class and the circumstances will know about the distance. I should have said the seas out by was not long seas like what I have seen in other waters; they were short, so we were better able to get about them. They were very high, and by their noise I thought they were strong. I for one thought it was as bad or the worst we could come through and live, but I had worse to come through, yes, and in an open boat. We have experienced worse, heard and read of as bad and worse, but this summer night of 1881 sticks to me more than any of the other happenings, why I don't know. I have been caught in a calm and without warning more than once since then.

The Blade of Heylor is a sandy point projecting from the west side of Ronasvoe and may be half way in the Voe. I said there was a lot of boats there. Yes, the Ronasvoe boats, they could not land at their station out by – they were there. There were boats from Fethaland and Uyea. Our station there was quite a crowd. These boats came early, some with daylight and some with the last of the daylight. All the boats from the three stations was on the mid- or trading ground, about 15 miles off. Some wir hauled their lines and were talking of shutting again. Some had a line or part of a line to haul when the wind came. They cut and took the very first of the weather. Being inshore they did the wisest thing; as bad as it came, the first was not the worst. That applies more so to inshore tide strings, etc. None of our boats got to our station. Two got into the east'ard of the Isle to Sandvoe about 10 p.m. They could not have got in that way later. One of the two boats who left the land with us was at the Blade when we came. When he came, or how he got on, I never got to know. If he was offshore and his lines fell among fish like us, he had to be thrown them, as he had not much fish ashore. One thing I know, wherever he was he would have hauled in all his lines before he shut out again; he would not haul in part like us. Hauling in part and shutting out was a system some men wrought on when opportunity offered. They had their ideas, such as, if fish is taking at night they may not take in the morning, and midnight is not good for fish in any case – whether a good system or a bad one I am not able to say. It suited us on this occasion as we had just anof of fish. The other boat that left the land with us did not come till 6 or 7 in the morning. He came to the Blade. I never got to know what kept him at sea, and what I have said about the other boat that left the land with us, the same applies to him.

When I came down to the Blade and joined our men in the forenoon, the boats were all way; they had gone to their different stations. The Ronasvoe boats had gone in the voe for home: they could not go to their station for the sea. We followed the other boats for our station at Uyea. It was still not fairly settled in the sea outside (there was a Ronasvoe boat missing). We came to our own station, cleaned up our fish and had it weighed. The market fish was one ton, and reckoning on the other we would have about one ton six hundredweight. I am saying this just to show the weight we had aft. This trimmed through the boat was trifling, but all being aft it put her starn much down. I came to find out that that was meant to keep her starn down and not to lift too much when pressed with the sail.

There was a boat missing from Fethaland, and we heard there was a good many missing from North Yell – Gloup. The people ashore came to have evidence of these boats being cast away in the vicinity of the shore, and blamed the night and darkness. But it might and could have happened with daylight. The Ronasvoe boat, he might have been west on the fishing ground. In any case, when he made sail he would know he had a fair run anof and to spare. With such weather the land could not be seen very readily even in daylight. There's no doubt this man passed no chance of keeping her east, for he would soon see what he was losing running seas. Some people may think he's run too much – he had to. He would never run a sea under the circumstances but the ones he had to; that is, he never would have put his boat into what he knew she could not stand until the last effort. They had evidence she was cast away in the vicinity of the Okern Heads looking for land, and mostly when land is looked for it's the high land. Men doing so could pass such a thing as the Ossa and never see it. However, he would see his position. Being in running trim, coming up further than a beam wind would be no use, the boat would not work above that; so to try his last chance – if he gets a chance to do this – would be to set everything light and alter his boat's trim. When that's done – if he gets the chance – the weather is too much for her: it's blowing a gale, and seas much too heavy for an open boat; she's close-reefed, and when he doadges to get to weather of a sea she goes by the broadside. So I cannot see that daylight would have saved them. As it was this good man knew perfectly well where he was making for; did his part well the same as those that got in; brought his boat to within a stone-throw of his port; but it had not to be.

The same would apply to the Fethaland boat. She was from the Easter Ayre. Coming ashore he too would have a fair run around the Stacks. Being on an easterly tack, his running seas would bring him to the wast'ard and bring him down on the strings between the Isle of Uyea and the Ramna Stacks. He probably thought there was no use trying her at the wind to get around the Stacks, and thought there might be a chance of getting into the Wester Ayre or Sandvoe. She could not do it, so you see this good man too was within a stone-throw of getting his proper way to the east'ard of the Stacks, but it had not to be. I knew one boat who came into the Wester Ayre; the time I don't know, but the people ashore seen her approaching the shore and it was a marvel she got in. It's needless to try and describe this way in to those that don't know it. I was told by people ashore that what they saw with the last daylight was it breaking in one sea from the Isle of Uyea to the Ramna Stacks.

The Gloup boat that came down our way, her wreck came ashore. There was evidence that she was cast away at sea, not on shore. I have thought a lot about her, and find he would be making for the mouth of Yellsound to the east'ard of the Ramna Stacks. Like the other Gloup boats he would be off shore. He knew his own place and he knew what like it was to take. All along the Yell shore to Whalfirthvoe, he could not take that: the sea would be breaking across it; he would know the course with the wind for his own place and would allow so much to the west'ard to be clear of Yell, and come in Yellsound; he would thus be on a westerly tack. There was evidence he was cast away outside in line with the Sounds of Uyea, so if he was making for Yellsound, which was wise anof, he was not much out on a long run – just about three miles; in ordinary weather that would not have been reckoned much. Yes, he had her at the wind: the bowling was hauled down. He would come down on Uyea and see the Isle of Uyea and the Ramna Stacks. He would be shorter rounding the Isle than the Stacks if she could do it; it would be the last effort keeping her on the same westerly tack, but she could not do it. But I think by what I have, that she was worked alright, as by what I saw I was in the opinion that she had been struck forat on the bow by a sea. The top of her stem and the gunwale aft past the tack were knocked off. This being the case mast and sail would go over the side, and most likely she would be partly water-logged. It would be then that this good man cut the weather shrouds and made himself fast in the boat. He could not have done that had the boat been altogether water-logged. The shrouds was longer cut than he could reach had they been standing. This and other evidence shows that the boat was broke in two, not crushed as she would be if rammed by a steamer. When she was full of water, she would be landed with a sea half-way on a aff-lying rock such as the Cloe, which forms the east side of the Little Sound of Uyea. When half on she would be left dry and break in two, the after half, where the body was, would drop to the lee side of the rock. It had not been otherwise in contact with other rocks that could show, and had not been tossing about. If so the body was likely to have been hanging over outside. It was just lying in a reclining position in the owes-room, where the shrouds is set on. It was found in the North Wick of Uyea. That's to the east'ard of the Isle and in line with the Sounds. I could give more details about this boat, but this may do, and if I am right in this good man making for Yellsound I think he did a very wise thing, and was surprised that more of the Gloup boats did not do the same, and although this one did not get through, others might and was likely to be all right. The mouth of Yellsound is a fine open sea, and when entering, coming gradually to the west'ard. So what I think is that this man did not misbehave in any way, but played his part well like others, but just like the others, it had not to be.

THE 1887 SNOWSTORM

A Northmavine Fisherman's Experiences Told by Himself (*The Shetland News.* 10th January, 1935)

The year 1887 was one of a period of years that a haddock [line] fishing was carried on around Shetland. The class of boats used were the Shetland four-oared boats measuring off and on about 11 to 12 foot of keel, [18-20 feet overall] with a crew of four. No doubt there were a few cases of bigger boats in some places, with more of a crew, and a very few cases of smaller boats with two or three of a crew.

Me and my brother [Laurence] and two other men had a boat and fished from Burravoe, North Roe. We were out at the fishing on the morning of the 9th December, and did fairly well. The weather was open and unsettled, with a very heavy sea running, but it was fishing weather. We arranged to go in the afternoon to work with a south tide. Me and my brother could only get one line ready, so I went and he stayed ashore. We did not like the appearance of the weather. The sun was too bright for the dead of winter, making the ground smoke with its heat and as the day spent, its appearance looked rather worse. The sea increased, and we were looking for a dirty night, but were not looking for what came.

So under the circumstances we stayed on our ordinary fishing ground, north and east, in Yellsound. There were two boats south-west of us, and one north of us. We were the furthest east, and we started to shoot our lines about 3 pm. When finished we pulled back to the buoy we started at. We call that 'rowing between'. We do this when it's day- or moon-light, as we think it's a better way of tiding our lines. Then we started to haul and were getting fish. We had no wind and were lying across the tide. I noticed something like mist coming from a north-east direction and going over the west land. The sky was thick and black out that way. Presently it took away from view the point of Yell.

Without warning a dry squall struck the boat and put her head where her stern was. She was very light, with nothing in her, and very light-wooded. We cut the line and turned up – head on. The next squall was snow, a blinding spindrift. We had to try for our voe, but we had to take it side on, and she was unworkable in that position under oars. If we kept away from the lumps we would come to lee of our voe, and with the sea on the shore we would have no landing. To keep her up to the lumps we would make no headway and would be drifting. We lay head to wind for a short time, and being exposed to the weather from the open sea, we had to do something, not so much hope [of survival] as in a summer wind. It was a case of having to run with the wind, and as the wind was then we would come down between Lamba Isle and Little Roe, on the Delting shore. We decided to run. My two mates took an oar each, and came on the mid taft. Running under oars the boat has to be managed the same as under sail. There's one advantage with oars that's not with a sail – when it's right to check her speed it can be done quicker with oars.

To begin with there were some suspicious [tide] lumps to watch, and in slanting them or avoiding them I tried to do that on the one side as much as the other in order to make something like a course with the wind.

I had not got on my oilskin, and when we were seated I would not bother the men to get it for me, and with only a small cap on, the water ran down my back and front and filled my boots and oil trousers. But I did not feel so bad while in the boat. We kept running for a considerable time; it was a long way for a small boat to run. All of a sudden she rose on a sea preparing to break. This was so unexpected that I had no chance to slew her head to either tail of the sea, but I let the helm swing loose and free. She rose like being clear of the sea, and had a swinging motion in her dive. She came a bit up to port and was thrown, falling on her starboard bow in a quieter [flatter] surface. Such a knock. It lifted me in the stern and threw one of the men off the toft in the room. She uprighted and continued her race. In a short time we came on the shore – a low-lying rocky shore with the sea going over the rocks and breaking on what appeared to be a beach above. They told me to keep her along a bit. They had given her a few strokes when one of these big waves on a lee shore rose outside of us. I slewed her head towards the shore. She got on the top of that wave, and strange as it may seem she stopped [stayed] on the top until it broke on the beach with her.

My version of that is that the pressure of wind on the boat was equivalent to the speed of the wave. We got her up a bit, and I found my oilskin washing through the boat, but I never found my mittens. We did not know the place where we had landed. We knew at first sight it was not where we thought we would come. We secured the boat with the lines we had in the foot of an open drain, and started to walk along the seashore. The snow was wet from the sea so it was not so bad. We came to a little pond in the beach, and one of the men had been brought up in Delting and he knew it. He said we were at Crougester Voe, Orka Voe. We had landed on Monaness. We would walk round the voe and he would know when to leave the shore to find the house of Orka. We did that, but did not find the house. Standing about for a bit, it was then I found it was freezing. I was wet through, with no mittens, bare face and neck, and a wet cap. In that state, with my feelings, I did not expect to hold out long. But I did not think it was because we were in Delting. I still thought we had done right by running for the most likely place of safety.

When one of the men fell up against a heap of manure, we knew we were near a croft. We all shouted together and the Smith people heard us up at Caldback, and came out with fire. We walked on the fire, and they treated us very kindly. I was the only one who needed dry clothes, and I was soon all right. We went to bed but could not rest. The weather was broken but was going very heavy squalls. The moon was up and between the squalls it was not so bad, so we decided to try and get to Northmavine. We would travel to the east side of Sullom Voe and might get across there. We got to Sullom Voe with a struggle, and came to the house of Arthur Anderson. His light was up, and he took us in and treated us very kindly. Arthur and his wife had been at a marriage feast and had just come home. Arthur went back to the house of the marriage and got whisky and gave us a drink of it, and also food. Getting across Sullom Voe was out of the question. The squalls were so heavy it would not be seamanly to put a boat afloat. Further, the boats were all under snow. But we had to try to get home. You see our people did not know how we were getting on, so we decided to try to travel around Sullom Voe by Brae, to Northmavine. Our sea boots were an encumbrance. These good people, Arthur Anderson and his wife, started with socks and odds and ends of clothes and served [wrapped] our feet and legs from the knees and down in such a way as to make sure our feet would take no harm. There were no roads to be seen, but some parts of the snow were so hard that we could walk on it. Other parts were soft, and we would go to the arm pits. We pegged at it and came to Swinister by the head of Ronas Voe in the afternoon. Mr. Hawick took us in and gave us a drink of whisky and food, and we got home with the last of the daylight, being 26 hours away, when we should only have been about four or five hours.

It took some doing, and but for the kindness we received on the way we could not have done it. On Saturday night, and next day, Sunday, all the boats and men about us were accounted for. The two boats to the south-west of us, one with three men, ran and came between Little Roe and Lamba Isle, to the Delting shore. They made a good job of it. The other boat, with four men, made for our own shore, and no doubt had a try for the voe. They were four men and a suitable boat, but they did not make the voe, [Burravoe] and came to lee of it. The wind may have shifted north a bit and misled them (and may have accounted for us coming east. We were [too far] east the length of the isle of Little Roe). They got into a gio. I cannot think they had that gio in view to begin with, as with daylight, and when we could see, there was no views of a safe landing at our shore outside the voe. But whether the wind shifted or not, my opinion is that they would have gone to lee whatever. In every such case in working a boat she goes to lee. But as their luck turned that way they saved themselves in the gio – a very bad place.

The boat north of us with four men would have worse weather than we had. She was in line and nearer the sounds of Grounie [Gruney]. It was bad enough where we were. We shall call them little seas – not so bad to deal with as tide lumps, but that boat had one advantage – they had a longer shore to work on to weather of the voe. They could afford to keep away and work towards the shore. They made the shore to the north of the holms of Burravoe. It would take careful handling to take a boat along that way in such weather. They got the voe and the boat to her own noost. Very well done, I always think. A boat and two men were working lines south of the Air of Skea. They had voes to lee; they did not get in one, but were driven in a gio where they barely had oar room, and they had to stay there till next day. The snow would accumulate on the gio top, and would break off and threaten to fall on the boat. How they held out without food and in the cold is wonderful.

When opportunity offered we went to Delting for our boat, and from where the boat stood I noticed the way we had come. We were working our lines with one of the Ramna Stacks partly locked up in Grounie Isle. From where the boat was standing that land mark was in the same position, and the baa at the east tail of Little Roe was about in line, so we had come straight down, and the sea I referred to above had to be that baa. It was the only sea to call dangerous; and, further, as we came south the seas got smaller. I rather felt [ashamed by] the idea of having come over a baa. It's very important that we do our utmost to know where baas are, so as to avoid them.

I had to console myself with the knowledge that the same had happened to a boat before, and a bigger boat although with a crew of seven, and a bigger baa, as the skipper related it to me, that case and ours was the same. The baa at the east tail of Little Roe is a very short distance from the Isle, and it had to be very thick when we did not see the Isle. It was like fog and snow mixed. The Isle would have shown white with a dark border, and be lying in a different position to any isle or land we might have come to or past, lying down [travelling] that way. Had we seen it we would have known it and we could have gone right up the voe.

I have never heard or known of any night like it with boats afloat. There was 17 lives lost, I think, mostly through cold. I did not wonder at that as in my own case of men getting wet through overlooking the importance of putting on oilskins and worse still, [men] pulling till overheated, and having to give in, their efforts being of no use. There were no lives lost up our way.

A DEFENCE OF THE HAAF FISHING

(*Manson's Shetland Almanac.* 1939)

The time came, when we got older, to go to the haff and mix up with the same fishermen we had the time with on the fishing station. We had to be saints in many ways. Some of the men took no notice what we said. Others were very strict in the way we spoke the names of different things, and we must not have a sea bath at the weekend, etc. But we often stole away and had a sea bath when it was not fishing weather. Yes! Lots of rules, too numberless to mention.

The boats about us all carried a boy and six men. The boy had an oar, and in still weather a man pulled two oars on the narrowest part of the boat. We boys had wages, our living, and so many boughts of fishing lines, and the boy could choose his boughts in any part of the drift. Some boys were only a season, others as far as three. We were fairly well paid, and went as a man if we chose to do so when we could stand up to a man's work. In fact, I know of a few cases of men who went as boys all their lives.

It was no trifling matter to be a man on one of those heavy boats in my time. They were an improved class of boats from those in my grandfather's time. This newer class was much heavier and fitted with eight oars, and the oars were never used but in still weather – all the sail in every case but working lines. Working lines was done with four men at the oars.

I know something about the older class of haff boats called sixaren, fitted with six oars, and off and on about seventeen or eighteen feet of keel; my father had an old black one for winter fishing. I was young, but I was old enough to see she could play her part well. We did well with her, and got a new one built. He did not do so well with the new one; what became of her I don't remember.

An Unst man had a boat of the same class and was out with her in the disaster of 1881. He was at sea through it all and came into Uyeasound about mid-day. These boats could not be beat at their size and it has been said that our forefathers did not sail them much. I know they were good under sail on any occasion. I am an old hand in open boats fishing the haff, etc., and as writers mostly paint it black, I am able to give you a true description of the life it was, and a bad job for these Islands when it was given up. These writers are, mostly people who know nothing about the haff or the life it was.

We found it a fine life, which I shall explain. Some people think it was the '81 disaster that did for the haff fishing. Not at all. There was a lot of haff going after '81, which was not so serious as some people make out. We in our parish had five stations with the weather as it was. The five stations were on the worst lee shore in Shetland – no entrance but one small one, and we lost two boats. When we consider the number of open boats which were afloat from the islands in July, 1881, and the loss of about 50 men, it is not much to compare with the disaster at Eyemouth the same year, 13th October 1881, of 189 fishermen drowned.

Can any of my readers mention a sea line of life where there has been less loss of life than in open boats? You must bear in mind that these open boats were afloat all the year round. The class of boats in the winter were the smaller boats. The haff fishing, or deep-sea fishing in open boats, commenced early in May and ended early in August. The state of the weather often made the time a week or so longer or shorter. The fishing time ran about from ten to twelve weeks, and the average trips to the haff were once a week. Thirteen trips would be the exception, and happened only once for the time given to my knowledge.

One of these trips to the haff occupied about 24 hours. Of course there were exceptions such as very still weather and shooting out part of a drift, which was called a second hail or with the wind off the land, which kept the boats longer in getting up to the land, such as tacking under reefed sail. That was the smaller number of times. The greater number of times it was 24 hours being one hail (set) of the lines. There were no dry and prepared lines so as to have a second set. The one drift was enough for the class of boat, and men would not run the risk of being without two nights' rest. There could not be more than three trips to the haff in one week, one night at sea, the other night ashore, and many a week went and no fishing weather.

During these windy weeks there was a lot of sleep and rest indulged in. But in those days we all, or almost all, could make and mend our own boots, and make and mend our own clothes, and every night when ashore there was sought and got fresh bait for our great lines in case of haff weather next day, so although there was rest, there was very little idleness. I have lifted over £20 for this short season and I have known men lift £26. Certainly I have known bad summers, when very little was done.

In preparing for the haff early in May, the crew went and put their lodge (hut) in order. These lodges had stone walls and were about the size of a crofter's house of floor space. They were roofed with thin turf divots called pones, and were mostly all thatched with straw. A lodge, and where the boat was moored, followed each other, and were handed down from father to son, or from skipper to skipper, for generations.

A dry stance was selected handy with where the boat was moored, and when the lodge was ready the inside was put in order. When cleaned out, seven feet of the inner end was set off for a shake (bed). This was for the crew. First was laid a layer of beach. Next was a thick layer of heather. Next a thick layer of straw. Each man brought his own bed-clothes and pillows. All the bed-clothes were sewn together with an opening left on the centre. This was in my time. In my grandfather's time one man found the bed-clothes.

At the foot of the bed at the centre is the fire, with a low stone wall between the bed and the fire. A chain and hooks came down from the roof for kettles and pots for cooking purposes. At the other end of the lodge and handy with the door was a raised platform for stowing dry lines on till required for the haff, two long seats running along each side of the lodge. With plenty of peats for firing, this was very comfortable and cosy with the cold weather in May, and cool with the hot weather about midsummer.

We got to our homes every week-end. When it was haff weather on the Friday, it would be late on the Saturday night and sometimes the early hours of Sunday, before we got home. When it was no haff weather on the Friday, we got home on the Friday night.

There was not so much lost time as I have experienced at other lines of fishing. As I have said, most of the men were handy men. Those were the days when wooden buckets were made and used, so we had men of a good many trades – coopers and carpenters who could build or mend a boat.

Now speaking from my own experience, we shall compare this life with in other lines of fishing. To begin with, I have always seen more views of safety in an open boat than I have seen in larger vessels. Our open boat under sail is a thing *alive* and only needs proper guidance. And for the life, take the decked sailing boats. The living accommodation was too small, a man could not get to his height where cooking had to be done, and the foot of the mast travelling through the centre of the place where it was lowered and set. And as we would have to come out of that hot, stuffy place, and go out in the worst weather in the spring of the year. Yes, and living in that conditions for months – some difference by living on a fishing station and going to the haff!

Then take the Faroe fishing in large smacks: being at sea for about three months and living under conditions similar to what I have described in the decked boats. I have never been in steam or motor at the fishing, but judging from what I know, I would take the steam or motor to be a worse life than in sail.

I did never wonder at men finding fault with the haff fishing. They were men that did not know about anything worse, and these men going to the haff were in the majority. Certainly as I have said, it's ill for our Islands that open boat fishing died out.

In describing a trip to the haff, up to about ten miles off the shore was reckoned the inshore fishing-ground. About 16 miles was reckoned the mid, or trading ground, off and on according to fish and weather. With suitable weather and few fish on the trading ground, fish was sought further off, up to 20 miles. The furthest offshore ever I was, and the old men said so too, was in the 1881 disaster, when we were four hours under sail to the land. Had it been clear weather we would not have been so far off, but as it was we had gone further than was intended.

I have read that open boats had "gone the land down" and as far as 70 miles. That has never been in my time, and I have my father's and grandfather's authority on that. They had been going further off since they got the bigger boats than ever they went with the smaller ones, which were in my grandfather's time and were not out of use in the first of my father's time. They had a rule not to go out of sight of land, and in fact it was seldom ever they lost sight of more than the low lands. Certainly there were mistakes in thick weather, but they always knew not to go out of bounds by the depth of the water. It would take over 20 hours to pull 70 miles, and over 40 to pull twice that: that's about four working days. We used to think pulling one working day stiff enough. These open boats could not fish at 70 miles unless with a very short line. Further, we all had to mind the want of rest; there was no chance of sleep in an open boat, and very poor provision for cooking. It was all very well for a 24 hours or so, and we could make up for what we lost in the way of food and rest, so 60 or 70 miles offshore is "bunkom". The men in my time were too wise to try nonsense of that kind, and the men before my time were wiser still with their open boats. They had boats the crew could manage with oars at sea, and could haul up on a beach. As for these bigger boats, it took two and sometimes three crews to haul up one of them, and best of all the crew could keep one of these smaller boats head to wind with their oars, and would give her every chance to live as long as they could hold out. It was not so with one of the bigger boats. When she fell off, oars could not take her head up.

A sea anchor is no comfort in an open boat. It is a comfort in non-dangerous weather but when it comes to dangerous weather it gives the boat no chance to live. There are a lot of evils, and the worst one is that the boat ranges too much, and when she should be head up she is nearly broadside on. Further, seas rise to break as high as her mast, and that is not a very high sea. When that turns over it would not take much of it to fill her. Some may think she will climb a breaking sea. She may if it is a small one. I know something about the use of a sea anchor and I would prefer the boat to have a loose head with a bit of sail. Every seaman knows that his sails are his life. Science will never bring in anything to beat sails for safety at sea, and sails are of most importance to open boats. I have been 15 hours tacking what was reckoned to be about 16 miles. I wonder how long it would take tacking 60 or 70 miles under the same circumstances. I have known boats tacking longer, but although disagreeable, it very seldom happened, and was little thought of.

Tacking under sail and running before the wind, the one is much different to the other. Running, they used to say, was the most dangerous. I could never see that when tacking in a bad sea under small sail. In running, there were three men to look out for the safety of the boat, two sailmen, as I have been used, one sailman proper, and a volunteer along with him. The one might be as good as the other. They were of course responsible men, but the man at the helm took the most responsibility of the three. He could make it much easier for the sailman if he inclined to do so. The sailman sat down to the halyards like sitting down to his own fireside, and I knew one who used to say, "Now, my good lady, give us a decent dance and I'll hold your bonnet."

I read in an article that the sailman sat with his face aft and watched the following seas (a following sea does not mean the sea is chasing the boat – seas do not travel). It is not common sense to say he sits facing aft. The sail is not fitted up for that. None of the three concerned looks aft. It's what the boat may run on to. I wonder if the writer knows of any sailmen who can manage looking aft.

I will describe a trip or two to the haff. I shall not describe the best, they were common enough and were followed with sport and pleasure. I shall not describe the very worst; they were very rare, only a very, very few times in a lifetime. They were overlooked and forgotten about. I will describe something between the two.

On a Monday early in May, we were on the fishing station, and ready for the haff. I was one of my father's crew. Haff weather did not offer till Thursday, when the fleet set out for the mid or trading ground with a light west wind. Every boat shot her drift. We used an anchor to ride at while tiding the lines and as a rule that was two hours. Before that time the wind had shifted to S.S.W. and started to blow fresh. When the anchor was in it was as much as we could do to take the buoys with four oars. When we got in our buoy and sinkers our line stood fast in the ground (bottom). The men carried the line away [broke it], hauled and held. In ordinary circumstances that would be a wrong way of working. There are different manoeuvres that would be carried out in still weather to get the line clear. One is to cut, bend on a buoy and grapple. What we had to do in this case was to make a tack to windward to get our mid buoy (buoy in the middle of our lines). We took in one reef and stood to the eastward far enough to fetch up to our buoy. We lowered, took in another reef, stayed, and came to the westward and fetched just a short distance to lee of our buoy. We could not take her with oars, so we stood on to stay and come to weather [windward] of the buoy and settle [drift down] on her. We lowered and had to take in a third reef, stayed, and the boat was laid for the land. She lay on her side and fetched up like a beauty. She had only about 3 cwt. of ballast. Some may think we needed these reefs as the boat was light. No. She would have needed the reefs even with weight. I know different boats that carried no ballast. We had to make a tack at the land to fetch our station. We lowered and had to take in a fourth reef. It was a high wind off the land. We got up about midnight, and although we were washed down with spray when we got off our oilskins our clothes were dry and in the hut we were comfortable.

Friday and Saturday there was no sea weather. Monday following, the weather was better, but not very suitable for our job. However, we set out, and the weather bettered. With the land-marks these older men knew exactly where the lines were left. Our first buoy was away too. She had ridden off the bottom. Our mid one was away too. She and her sinker had taken the bight out of the lines and gone with them. So we lost two buoys, and with the bight we lost about six boughts of lines, so in this case we had to grapple. We had some job, but we got fast in one half and then the other half. We got ashore next day, Tuesday. Our lines were out of repair and had to be carefully examined in case of chafe or half-cuts on the bottom, so it happened that in a week's time we were nothing behind other boats. Nothing more happened out of place to us that season.

Jeemsie Laurenson

Jeemsie Laurenson.
Photo by Bobby Tulloch

James John Laurenson, known to all as Jeemsie, was born at Aithbank, Fetlar in 1899; one of a family of nine. Falsifying his age to join the Royal Navy in World War I, he served in the Northern Patrol, but lived the rest of his life on the family croft at Aithbank with his brothers and sister. He was probably Fetlar's strongest man of the 20th century, renowned for his feats of strength such as raising the blade of a sixern's oar off the ground while grasping its loom with only one hand. Jeemsie was an outstanding story-teller and an authority on every aspect of Fetlar – history, genealogy, place names, people, folklore, sea lore, music and all else, which he willingly imparted to the many visitors who came from far and wide to learn from him. Between 1959 and 1965 he wrote a number of articles for the 'New Shetlander' including the series of seven 'Sixern Days'. He had a unique style with the pen, technically correct, very proper in expression, and, endearingly, favouring the royal 'We'. He died in 1983.

"FRAM ON" IN THE STORM OF '81

(*The New Shetlander*. No. 53, 1960)

Their anchor now is cast, within the harbour fair,
They will not row their boats again,
Nor yet close-reef their sails
(Lines written by a Yell man at the time of the Gloup disaster).

A story of the sea has special attractions for us Shetlanders, especially if it has something to tell about the Haaf fishermen of the past generation, and the fine boats they sailed. It is good to know that the interest lingers on. This is amply shown in the interest aroused by Mr. A.T. Cluness' series of articles on the 1832 gale recently published in *The New Shetlander*. Mention in the concluding article of a Fetlar boat at sea in the storm of '81 has prompted me to string together a few more details of that night when many boats out on the fishing grounds were overtaken by the sudden storm and ten boats and 58 brave men failed to return.

We are fortunate in having an excellent account of the Fetlar boats from notes taken down from Thomas G. Hunter and George Garster whose father was one of Thomas Tait's crew.

All five Fetlar boats at sea that night returned safely. The Isbister men's 18-foot boat *Matilda* skippered by William Isbister, out on the North Haaf, was first in. The Tresta crew, in a hired sixern, with their young skipper Laurence Bain, then aged 33, at the helm, made a good run in to Hubie. The Coutts men of Funzie in a 19-foot boat *Margaret* on the In Haaf, only seven miles out, had much the worst time getting in. Having landed a big catch the day before, they had dumped their ballast, and as it was a calm day when they left their moorings, they set out for the fishing grounds light. They were setting their lines when the storm broke. James Coutts, skipper, cut and buoyed the lines. Knowing they could not sail her, they doused the mast and took to the oars. Coutts was badly placed, being on the southerly grounds with wind and tide against him. The crew had a hard struggle, but being strong men in their prime, they made it, getting up to the Holms, soaked to the skin with spray and sweat.

Another boat, the *Maggie*, with a Hubie crew skippered by Irvine Park, was out at the "Auld Fram Haaf," twenty miles E.N.E. of Hosta Head. Park (said to be as good as ever held a helm), decided to try for the lines. Like Tait, he hauled to windward, placing his two strongest men in the fore-room to haul, with the other four at the oars. After a four hours' struggle they succeeded in getting the lines [aboard]. He weathered the Bound of Skerries [the Bound Skerry] on the first tack in and on the second he weathered Muckle Skerry. The way skipper and crew handled their boat was long spoken about by the fishermen of Aith who watched the boat next morning beating up the firth. With sail reefed down and well set, and foaming at the bow, throwing the spray above her horn [stemhead], she made a good picture of a sixern showing her paces. When they took her in to the wooden tress [landing stage] at Hubie she was frothing at the fore-room clinks.

It can be said that in a N.W. gale these Fetlar boats, and especially those out on the southerly grounds, were as badly placed as any of the boats at sea that night. With faraway Norway the nearest land to lee, the boats had to be punched into it.

We now move on to the last boat, the *Spray*, skipper and owner Thomas Tait. His crew was as follows: Arthur Tulloch, Aith; James Hart, Kirkhouse, later Feal; Jacob Garster, Littaland; David Hart, Funzie; James Charles Hart,

Funzie (on his first trip to Fram Haaf). The adventure of the *Spray* became the local talking point with skipper and crew coming in for much praise. To be caught in a storm when 40 to 50 miles out in the North Sea and to drive their boat for thirteen hours on to Bressay, scarcely having to draw the pump on her, while barques and smacks were scudding for shelter inshore, was considered an outstanding performance of seamanship.

On recounting their adventure to the shop manager at Aithbank, Tait said that his concern was that if the wind westered on them they might miss Shetland altogether. When asked what he would have done in that event, he said "We would just have had to keep going till we made the Scotch coast."

Of the many boats he built Tait considered the *Spray* his best job. He had run her for two seasons before '81, and in that time he must have sized up her possibilities. When asked by Mr. Garriock of Aithbank how he was pleased with his new sixern and how she behaved at sea, he said, "when I couldna mak da land wi her, wi David Hart at da tows – it's not a good day." He had a high opinion of his towsman, and always said in later years that never once did David do the wrong thing, and never needed a telling.

But it is time to get on with the story. We begin with the *Spray* lying to her lines with the crown of the Muckle Pobie" (Saxavord) down to sea level. To quote Jacob Garster: "We had set off and were lying to the lines; the weather was fine but the swell from N.W. was getting deeper. We got up the fire kettle and had a bite of grub. James Hart, who had a watch, said it was 5 p.m. After a bit it clouded over and some rain fell with bats of wind. This cleared and it fell calm again. Soon after this we saw black water to N. and N.W., and in a short time the gale was on us.We had to press down on our sou-westers till we got the strings tied under our chin. We laid out the oars and took her head up. We lay on with the oars for a time, then the skipper said: 'Well men, we are before it now. We will just have to do the beat we can. We will see what we can do with the lines.' Tulloch said, 'Lines indeed! We'll never get a span.' The skipper said, 'We will have to get more weight in her before she can carry sail with this wind.' We then took the buoy and began hailing. James Hart and Tulloch hauled in the fore-room. We others andooed [rowed slowly] up to the lines. The skipper told them to pay off to her when the biggest waves made ahead, and told us at the oars to do the same.

"The calmness of the skipper was a great help to us and to the boy off with us for the first time. He kept telling us to take our time and not to oppress ourselves unduly.

"We were not taking any heavy water, but when the seas struck forrad the spray rained over us. We at the oars were not so bad, but the men hailing were having a hard time hauling her up to the lines. After lifting the mid buoy and hailing the fourth packie [line], the skipper said we had enough weight with the wet lines, and told the boys to cut away the rest of the fish.

"When we got the rest of the lines we kept her up while the boys reefed the sail and trimmed her up for sailing. Then we laid her by and gave sail. The skipper, however, was not pleased with a reef-point in the belly of the sail so we had to run her to take down and re-tie the reef point. Even under the mast she was foaming at the bow and when she fell in, the broken water was nearly up to the lee tack bores. When the reef had been re-tied, we lifted on her again. The skipper had to take her up at once to head two angry seas. When he was aware that the way was off her he said 'Ship an oar at the fore taft in case she falls by on me.' We had just got it shipped when a wave struck the blade and snapped it at the kabe. The skipper said, 'Lay out another, oars are not much good to us tonight'."

Having given the reader and idea of what it was like at sea that night we will now give the main account in brief. It may be interesting to hear what Arthur Tulloch, a sailing ship man had to say: "I did not feel altogether afraid, I just resigned myself and hoped for the best. But when I watched Tait first heading and then running in that wild black night, I did not think we had a chance."

Daybreak gave land on the weather bow. Tait said: "If you see land that should be Skerries." Hereabouts they ran into rough tide-water. To quote Garster again: "We had to run her over two heavy seas. She took them well, with just a swittle of water over both sides." One heavy lump struck her on the bow and smothered her forrad, but she sailed on.

They were gradually making up with the land now and, getting smoother water, Tait could sail her. As he himself said: "When I could take the sheet off [slacken] her and give her a chance she took off like a white maa." Then they saw land ahead, which turned out to be Bressay. When they had entered Aithvoe, to quote Garster again, the skipper said, "You needna row her right up the voe, boys. We will just have a blow [rest] here for a bit." The boys looked to one another, and David Hart said "Tammy, when God has given dee land why does du not tak it?" The skipper replied, "The same God that broucht wis here can bring wis hame."

So out of the voe they sailed again. The wind had moderated a little, but they still had to carry the four reefs, and it was not until north of Whalsay that they shook out two. When half up the firth they gave her full sail. With her white painted bottom, the *Spray* could be spotted at a distance, and on sighting her some of the young folk flitting peats in Lambhoga went out on the headland to give the boat a wave and cheer.

On seeing the waving Tulloch said, "See yon silly fools, little do they know what we have been through." Tait replied, "let them wave, poor things, we are glad to see them waving. We may never have been here for them to wave to."

On reaching their moorings at Aith the sail fell to the mast – calm. We will conclude by noting the individual comments of the crew when they set foot on terra firma again.

The skipper: "Sometimes I did not think we would touch a stone on Shetland."

David Hart: "Three times the boat complained sairly."

Jacob Garster: "We are here, but sometimes it lay in little room."

James C. Hart: "I was a bit faerd at first but it passed off."

Arthur Tulloch: The Lord forgive a wife who keeps a man home and makes him go to this calling and stops him from going on a ship where he has 'wid' and iron to preserve him."

THE SIXERN DAYS Part I

(*The New Shetlander*. No. 63, 1962)

We have been reading in the magazine lately about how we could have changed, and haven't, or should have changed and wouldn't, which of course is much the same thing. However it seems that we are not likely to change much in our traditional inclination for the sea and boats, be they pushed along by sail, motor, or just the old oar and "humlibaund."

And so it is, that the young men of today will enjoy a day well spent among the "olicks" as well, if not better than, their grandfathers. And despite a spot of doubt about such things as Census Statistics we see more "whillies" on the beach now than we can ever remember formerly. And what boats they are! Those brought in from the "Bonny Isle" take some beating – one can scarcely detect the board scarfings [scarf joints] . What is more, the builders have built to the original Shetland model lines, and if they were brought up, at their overall ratio, to a keel length of 21 feet, they would put up a good show against the best among their sires of last century.

We may safely assume that it is many moons ago since the double-ender became the vehicle of movement across the voes and sounds of the islands.

Sixern at Brough, Fetlar, pictured in 1989. Sadly she has been left to disintegrate and little now remains. *Photo by Charlie Simpson*

As the settlers increased so would the boats, and later, when the islanders began building on their own, then boards and ribs, in sets, were brought across from Norway. We may assume that the early builders would have depended on trial and error before a good boat was produced but when a good job was forthcoming it would be tried out and further improved on, and so the process went on until a near-perfect plan was arrived at, which met with general acceptance by the builders.

Different Models

It did however happen, perhaps more by accident than intent, that there was a decided departure from what had proved to be the best all-round design. But where this happened the boat was never quite so good. We are fortunate in having a few interesting details of two Fetlar sixerns that support the fact. One of these was a 21-foot sixern purchased from Mossbank – *The Queen*. She differed from the other boats in that her keelrunners and sules [lower planks] were up to a vertical and she was sharp at the bow. When Thomas Tait was asked what he thought of her, his comment was: "Well, shü'll sail." And how right he was. She was the *Cutty Sark* of the Fetlar boats, and could do more than hold her own with the herring boats. But her crew did not like her. She was not a good boat in bad weather, and with her excessive grip in the water she lacked buoyancy and failed to lift well to the side wave. This defect was shown coming in from the haaf in a beam wind, with a heavy catch of fish and wet lines, when the boat took water over the side to excess.

The other one was just the opposite. This sixern, the *May*, was built by Thomas Tait and owned and skippered by James Petrie, Setter. Tait, who was very particular with his work, was against using the planking, which was a kind of redwood and not pliable. The result was that this boat was too "gutsy" and too bluff in the bow. Skipper and crew did not like her. She was heavy "on the routh" [under oars] and poor on a wind. This goes to show how essential it was to plank up with an eye on getting the best possible compromise.

An Outstanding Sixern

Let us now see how the good boat wins through when condiitions are almost at danger level. An outstanding sixern, Lerwick built, was the *Alabama*. She was skippered by Laurence Bain, Tiptobie, and had a Tresta crew. On one occasion the crew hauled their nets full up with herring, and three nets had to be cut away. Their position was south-east of the Snap, with a freshening south wind and a choppy sea. Looking overside, the skipper finds himself with just a few inches of freeboard. Can he do it? The *Alabama* has never let him down, but perhaps he is asking too much this morning. One sees a trace of anxiety while he is measuring his chances. But he will have to try. Calmly he gives his orders, "Clear the mast room [of herring], take a stead [stance], and break in the head of the water keg for a bailer. Hoist the full sail, and don't lower to her." She races along towards the Snap. The pump is choked with herring but the keg and owskerry can keep her. Deep as she is, she is doing well. Then with Stream Tonga abeam, she beats the tide water. Her performance must have impressed the fishcurer up from Lerwick, as he watched her coming in through the mouth of Aith, for turning to Mr. Garriock, he said: "Show me the man who has handled that boat loaded like that."

Few of these boats now survive, and it is rather sad to think that they, who were the thoroughbreds among all boats, are now a thing of the past, and almost forgotten. We in Fetlar can still boast of two.

The one at Hubie, formerly used as a flitboat, is the better model, and having been fitted with extra ribs, has kept shape well. Taken all-round, she may be considered a good specimen of the haaf sixern, and having a keel length of 21 feet, is of the size most common in these boats. It is interesting to recall that the best of the Fetlar boats were of a similar size – *Maggie*, *Spray*, *Onward*, *Alabama*, *Hawk*, *Queen*, while the pair, *Mary* and *May* – were 22 feet.

We may as well let the young folks who may be interested have a list of the island's grand old skippers who knew all the tricks of the game – Laurence Hughson, Hubie; Thomas Tait, Skerpigarth; Irvine Park, Beala; James Petrie, Setter; Arthur Brown, North Dale; Laurence Bain, Mioness, Funzie. Writing down the name of the latter raises a smile. He was head elder on one of the churches and was a pious man. Having the ability to preach a sermon, he taught himself to speak a very good form of English. He was known as the "pushing skipper," and more often than not, was top for the season. Very often, with uncertain weather, when the crew had assembled at the beach, someone would venture to say: "Jeems, tink you is it wadder? It looks as if it wis kinda takkin up." He did not take long to come away with his observations: "Then all the more need for us to make haste to get off before it comes. And He, who does not let the sparrow fall, will take care of us."

Naturally, one would hesitate to attempt to make comparison between these good boatmen who knew their job and gave of their best to what was an arduous calling. But perhaps the young folks may some time ask me: "Who would you fancy to sail you home on a bad night?" I might be a bit biased here, as I have always had a sort of admiration for one. Well? Yes, it would be the Beala man – Irvine Park. His crew always told how well he sailed them home in the gale of '81. He was badly placed, being on the south grounds of the Auld Fram Haaf, with Fetlar showing as three small holms. The two experienced fishermen who reefed the sail in the forehead just though it could not be done, to force the boat into breaking seas high above them, while the boat itself was ballasted down with fish and the wet lines. But after shipping the rudder and putting on his mittens he told the crew to give her the four-reefed canvas and to be of good courage as he hoped, with the help of a higher power, to bring them home. Then he set her into it, right in her teeth. She reeled and shook, but she had to take it. He knew it had to be Fetlar or Norway. His new Lerwick-built sixern, the *Maggie*, got a try-out that night! He nose-dived her into three heavy seas with such force that the two men sitting nearest the bow looked to see if the bow had caved in. They told him later that she was bubbling at the clinks [nailheads] and landings [seams] with the pressure. They all gave the skipper full marks right on to the end of their days, for the way he sailed them home on that bad night.

Arthur Brown was another who could handle these boats, and when he had the round stick on his shoulder the word "fear" was very much in the abstract. James Petrie was another who could make them dance with their reefs tied in. But we must not forget the man from Skerries, Laurence Hughson. What he didn't know about it was not worth knowing. And, of course, readers will have heard something of Thomas Tait in former articles. Laurence Bain was another topper who could yank them along. But we must not forget our own Aith men who in the *Queen* shook out the reefs and beat William Stewart's sixty-footer, the *Marjory Stewart*, on a beat in from the haaf. But Stewart was very sporting about it and offered to buy her.

We recall asking Doctor Peterson at Hubie one night to what he attributed the endurance and good nerves of the Shetland haaf men. We did not have long to wait for his answer – "The meal and the liver."

PART II

(*The New Shetlander*. No. 64, 1963)

It has been said by our best authorities on these things that, for sheer seaworthiness, the Shetland sixern was second to none among all boats. To some this may seem a bold claim, so it may be interesting for us to try and figure out just how good "old Blakka" really was.

In one or two discussions which we recall having had with merchant seamen we got an impression that they would just as well sit it out in the North Sea in a ship's lifeboat. Strangely, and with all their knowledge of seacraft, they seemed somehow to have missed the point. Their lifeboat may do as well, or perhaps better with a side drift or when riding to a sea anchor, or dodging head to wind under oars, but they would be equally safe in a fish kist, if high enough in the sides and with close seams. But they would be a sitting target for the sea, nothing more. Their craft would be lacking in its potential to forge ahead, under canvas, against a strong offshore wind, to bring them to safety. The sixern was unique in that it could, and did, sail through rough waters that would have tested much larger craft, and often at speeds that seemed incredible.

The Storm of '81

One instance is shown in the experiences of one of the west side boats out in the '81 storm. This sixern, in a run into Ronas Voe, had a speed average of 9¼ knots. That speed could have been reached in a fast sailer driven to her uttermost in smooth water. But the performance becomes all the more remarkable considering that the boat was "buxin" her way through waves up to danger level, and at times run off course.

These old double-enders were fine boats. They proved themselves worthy of the skill of those who fashioned them. Never was speed, buoyancy and all-over seaworthiness so happily blended. We learned much about these boats from first-hand accounts of their performance in the storm of '81. True it was a grievous loss at North Yell where ten boats failed to return; but the boats had little chance. It was believed that they arrived in at about midnight, when the storm and darkness was at its height, and so would have been at a great disadvantage in getting through tide-waters on a weather shore whipped up by the gale to danger level. Even with daylight to help them, the two boats *Agnes* and *Minerva* had to throw out broken livers to help them through.

It is interesting to note that boats of the keel length of 21 feet, which appears to have been the most common, sailed well in the storm. We like to remember that the *Spray* and *Maggie*, that put up a wonderful performance in a dead beat all the way from distant fishing grounds and so provided us with useful data which shows that these fine boats could do wonderful things when in highly competent hands. Still, it was found that the bigger boat with higher freeboard fared better. This seems to be made clear when it is recalled that the island's largest boat, the *Southern Air*, sailed through the area where the boats had failed, without any appreciable difficulty. It is believed that this sixern was the largest in the North Isles. She had a keel length of 24 feet, was full built, and as many of the Yell folks will be aware, was owned and skippered by one of the North isles' greatest sixern men, Daniel Brown of Basta.

The Skipper's Role

As in all ships the skipper's role is all-important. All these fine seamen who were out on that stormy night rose to the occasion and acquitted themselves in a way that we like to remember, although dimmed by time. They upheld the traditions of bravery of their sires who sailed the ships with the high head and the fintail. and their coolness and ability was an inspiration to their crews.

There were one or two isolated instances where, but for their skippers at the helm the crews would not have got home so well. Strangely, we detect a slight trace of uneasiness in the boats which had two skippers of exceptional ability to see them through. A case in point was on the flagship herself, Thomas Tait's *Spray*, with our island's greatest skipper in command. One of the best hands, Tulloch, insisted that the boat should be headed for land, ballast or no ballast. He did well at the hauling and did not spare himself, but he kept on reminding the skipper they were a boat-load of madmen and were sitting in the North Sea tempting Providence. But things improved a lot when Tait said politely but firmly that it was for him to say when the lines would be cut, and told him to peg away at it and to remember that the first duty of a seaman afloat was to keep calm in the face of adversity. The other skipper of the Tait standard was Robert Bruce, Baltasound. His men didn't like the idea of hauling when he pointed out that he needed more ballast for sailing. Nor were they over happy when he gave out the order to lay out the oars and lie-to, as he wanted light to take her through the tides of Skaw and Lambaness. These, and probably similar instances in other boats, go to show how much depends on the leader and how essential it is to act when he has the know-how, regardless of lesser considerations.

Sixern v. Steamer

Well, we seem to have wandered a bit from our subject, which was to try to see if we can decide whether "Blakka" was all that good in a seaway. We are therefore going to be quite complimentary to her, and compare her performance in a gale with that of her big iron sister, a steamer, in a less violent gale. The steamer was the old *Earl* [*of Zetland*], which went out to search for the smack *Columbine* adrift in the North Sea with Betty Mouat on board in 1886. Captain William Nicolson reported on his return to Lerwick, after the *Earl*'s fruitless search, "We were about sixty miles off the land. The wind blew very strong from the west; the sea was terrific. The day was one of the worst I have ever been at sea in. The sea was frequently breaking over our head. In at the land no one could form any idea how strong it was out at sea."

The sixern in this instance was the boat mentioned earlier on – the *Spray*, skippered by Thomas Tait, out in the storm of July 1881. From the best possible information given by people who had clear recollection of both memorable events, the '81 gale was by far the stronger, more especially from twelve midnight till two a.m. when the storm was at its height.

Now let us compare their respective situations. Nicolson was sixty miles out: Tait was fifty. Not much in it where wave crests are concerned. Nicolson had west wind: Tait north-west. Again pretty even. The *Earl* had to nose her way back in a gale for a distance of sixty miles. The *Spray* had to do likewise for 68 miles, making land at Bressay. The *Earl* had daylight to search and return to port. The sixern had to do her hardest sailing in the semi-darkness of the storm.

Nicolson speaks of conditions being very rough, with the sea breaking over their head. In short, he gives an overall impression that his craft was just about getting plenty. Now let us see how the little 'un, with the low side and open top got on, that sailed the same water five years before in a stronger gale, in near darkness. So we will join her in our imagination at midnight, when she is having her worst. The skipper has told the crew that if they were to make the east coast of Shetland he could not afford to run and advised those who had the best oilskins to take windward seats. It may be interesting to hear what Jacob Garster had to say; "Tammy took her up to one sea which I thought he should have run. She fell in heavy and was smothered forrad. David said: 'Tammy shü's complaining.' The skipper replied, 'Shü'll just have to complain, David. Shü'll have to take it and mebby more with it'."

Well, that doesn't sound like a skipper in despair. He is prepared to head all that comes, and is not upset when she takes a bow spray or reels a bit. He knows his craft has a good margin on the right side and, if need be, could take "more with it"! So, after her beat to land, having covered a distance of 68 miles and taken a relentless buffeting, she reaches Bressay. How has she taken it? Her rakki [traveller] had ground out a gouge in her mast that people looked at long after the fearless Viking had gone to his rest. She had been pressed so hard that the froth that had oozed from her clinks and landings were making her tarred bowboards look white. She had sailed through a storm almost twice as bad as her big iron sister. Yet withal, they did not have to draw the pump! That settles it for the Shetland sixern.

Fetlar's Greatest Skipper

So may we always be proud when we think of our island's greatest sixern man, Thomas Tait, who won great acclaim for his achievements on one of them, the *Spray*, built by his own hands. Of course he was no ordinary person. He was a man with a remarkable head-piece, and could have gone far in any calling. He often said that a good deal of the success in building a good boat lay in getting her bow to a correct pattern to pull and sail, and that the ideal should show a tendency to slice to windward. A boat should not be drawn at the tack knees, nor should she fall in to spout it green at the tack bores. Of the sail he had this to say – "When I reef, I reef. No use putting a single reef in a sixern's sail. If she needs reefing give her a double reef, and the boat should have command of the sail and not the sail have command of the boat: and never leave it to chance when at the helm."

PART III

(*The New Shetlander.* No. 65, 1963)

Readers of the previous article may recall that much of it was about the adventures of the haaf boats in the storm of '81. We mean now to include a few details of the greater storm of July, 1832, which took heavy toll and struck a shattering blow to the fishing industry, when seventeen boats were overwhelmed and 105 men perished. It was generally believed that the storm was without parallel in wind force for midsummer, while it continued without abatement for three days, causing damage inland, particularly to growing crops. On looking up some records we find that Fetlar was again fortunate and, although quite a number of boats were out from Urie and Funzie, only one boat failed to return. But it was a near thing for some of them, and several of the crews were so exhausted that they needed help to draw up their boats.

The missing boat, which was manned by a Funzie crew, was reported as having been seen pulling under oars, with the mast laid down, and appeared to be making headway. But in a gale blowing the tarpaulins and steepled fish down over the beaches, the crew would have had no chance whatever of getting up to the land. In fact, the last two boats to get into Funzie landed half their crews at the point east from the beach with bowtows laid double to pull the boats in along the shore towards the beach. The men who were in these two boats handed down what seems to be a rather remarkable story, which they told in after years that they owed their lives to one among them who had had a warning of the impending disaster.

One can imagine that it would not have been easy for him to divulge his warnings when he was known to be a man renowned for bravery to the point of recklessness. But, having had the double warning, he felt he would have to do something about it. He was last to arrive at the beach, and the skipper said something about him keeping them waiting. It was then he dropped his first hint by saying he was in plenty of time that morning. His second indication came when the lines were ready to be set for the third haul, and he told the others to unbend [untie] his "pakki" [set of lines; between 16 and 20 'buchts' of around 100 metres each]. It seemed that the skipper was rather surprised to hear such words from the one of whom it was least expected, and he pressed him to say what was wrong. He replied "There will be many a pakki set today that won't be hauled." That did it! The skipper told the crew to get out the oars and pull to their ranksman – the other boat. On hearing their decision the other skipper said he was coming with them. Both boats got in just in time.

Serious though the losses were in '32, the fishermen refused to be beaten. They accepted their setback as part of the risks that had to be taken following what was , after all, an arduous calling. The industry soon picked up again, and although many of the young able-bodied men of the islands were joining the Greenland whaling fleet, the number of boats steadily increased, till the haaf fishing reached its peak in the middle of the last century.

It would appear that the industry as a whole had its shady side in that the remuneration of these "toilers of the deep" seemed to have kept at a surprisingly low level. The terms imposed by the landlord curers were hard and heartless, in fact, little short of serfdom. After a time the lairds were superseded by merchant curers, many of whom supplied boats and lines on the "half-catch" principle. Although not everything to be desired, the arrangement was a step forward for the fishermen. The purchase price of £16 for a new sixern would not be killing nowadays, but at that period it would have been a princely sum and hard to raise. But after a time, due to better terms, the crews were able to purchase boats on a joint-ownership basis, which was a further improvement.

It is a well-known fact that, with a further loss of men and boats in the storm of July, 1881, the end of the sixern era was hastened on. Fishing on the distant grounds practically ceased and became confined to the inner grounds. There were signs of a depletion of fish, due to increasing numbers of large decked craft with curing facilities on board, and against these the smaller boats were at a disadvantage.

There is a good deal of material available giving details of the fishermen's rations, cost of lines, wear and tear, etc., but these may not be interesting. But we may add a brief reference to the price paid for the fish. It appears that it remained at a flat level over a long period at 5/- per cwt, headed and cleaned. There was a rise to 6/-, but that only came when the industry was nearing its close. Sometimes it was a fluctuating business. Curers were known to declare that they had struck a bad market and couldn't pay the agreed price, so the fishermen had no option but to take what they could get. The old folks told about one firm that got a lease of ground at Aith to set up a herring curing station. Smacks arrived, laden with the necessary equipment. Gutters were enrolled and nets supplied on hire at easy terms. Soon the place was a hive of activity and, as the manager walked up and down along the tiers of barrels, he kept repeating "Fire or water might destroy us but that is not within the power of man." But, alas, the klondyke was short-lived. A fourareen sailed into Aith at the end of the week with the dismal tidings that the firm had gone bankrupt.

But of course, life had its brighter side. The folks were happy and contented with their lot. It was a time of bustle and activity. The old folks always spoke about the Saturday evenings at the beach of Aith at the time when the curing was carried on by Hay & Ogilvy [Hay & Company?] and supervised by their capable manager, James Garriock. It was during that period the industry had its "Indian summer." The fishermen got a fair deal and were encouraged to do their best, and there was an all-round stimulus to the industry. Another point on the bright side was that quite a few of the fishermen had a credit balance in the hands of the merchant curers. After what has been said by many writers on the subject, this may sound like romancing, but entries in the account books of Smithfield can support this claim.

PART IV

(*The New Shetlander*. No. 66, 1963)

The foremost attribute of the sixern, which won her pre-eminence was that she had the ability in bow and belly to forge ahead in turbulent waters, where other types of open boats would have fared poorly. In fact it was when stepping out under a reefed sail, throwing the spray above her horn, that she was at her best.

But there were times, in the variable nature of the weather in these northern waters, that the boats were caught in high winds and through lack of ballast could not give sail. In these circumstances it was a case of riding to the lines, or dodging head to wind under oars. A safety measure known to have been taken when conditions were extremely bad was to hang the sail over the bow with the yard in the water, with tack and sheet secured to the tack bores. The idea was that the force of the wavecrests breaking on the canvas was somewhat spent before striking the bow. But while we have the names of several fourareens where this was done, and proved most helpful, we have no information of it having been resorted to in the sixerns.

Heavy Weather Tactics

Another timely precaution, well known to the haaf men was "bruckin da livers," which were dropped over to smooth the waves. This old-time stratagem was helpful when boats laden down with big catches were passing through these fierce tide-streams, where the going was tough and required skill to win through. All the fishermen had these dangerous waters to contend with in their course to the stations. The Unst men had a bad area at Lambaness; the Yell men at Gloup; and the Snap was a difficult part for the Fetlar men.

There does not seem to be any information of any loss of boats coming through the Snap. The only boat that we have heard of that had a narrow escape was a fourareen loaded with peats. For a time things looked serious. It was a case of "man bid man" at dumping peats and bailing. The old fishermen knew of a part where the tide-stream forked to give a smoother area, known as "da slap". The spot was found by medes, and the boats were steered through in rough weather. But we do not know the landmarks and is a pity that this useful bit of information has been lost.

A very early photograph by C. Spence shows sixerns drawn up at Aith haaf station, Fetlar. Thought to be in the early 1870s. *Shetland Museum and Archives*

We like to recall the yarns which we had with the old fishermen who sailed in the haaf boats, and who could remember the station at Aith in full swing. To us, the most remarkable of their stories were about certain boats coming in from the distant grounds with heavy catches in weather conditions where it seems almost impossible. It can be understood that with increasing wind the conditions on a weather shore could be quite nasty. Even at a sailing speed of seven knots it would have taken over six hours on the run in. They told of one of the sixerns, skippered by Arthur Brown, which came in with her shroud bores almost dipping. When nearing the Snap and seeing the conditions before them, the crew told later that they would have bet "da best coo in da byre" that she'd never do it. But only a Shetland sixern could perform feats like these. She stood alone.

The method of working the square sail when running in heavy seas is more or less well known. It was then that the towsman was as important as the skipper. The sail was hoisted to run from the wave, and lowered when on top. The towsman would begin lifting when the wave had rushed past the foretaft. He could tell by his foot on the board and by her sound how she was doing. Sail would be reduced when she was travelling to excess.

Fishing Medes

On looking up some notes, we seem to have a fair amount of information giving distance and bearings of the haaf fishing grounds of Fetlar. Perhaps the younger readers may be interested to have a few details of the farthest-off ground, when only the tops of the highest hills were in sight. This distant ground – the Fram Haaf – was more often termed the "Ocean" and is approximately fifty miles off. Thomas Tait often spoke with the skipper of the schooner *Ariel* which often passed that way trading to Bergen. He made out Tait's outer buoy to be over fifty miles from Strandbrough Ness. It works out almost the same, taking the speed under oars. The speed of a sixern of about 28 feet of waterline was about 3½ m.p.h. It took thirteen hours pulling from Hosta Head to set Saxavord down to the "Vaut," a mark high on the hill by which the inner buoy was streamed. Add five miles of lines, which makes it 50½ miles.

With the close of the haaf term in August, the sixerns were drawn to their winter quarters, and the fourareens launched and fitted out for the handline fishing. And, given good weather in the fall, landings were often quite good. There was keen rivalry between the crews "kemping" out to these famous ling seats, where it was said the best fish were taken. It may be added that four ling, headed and gutted and weighing 1 cwt., was considered good going. It seems remarkable that several of these fish-beds were never known to fail. Although the boats may have been on the grounds for days on end, they returned with good catches.

We find a wonderful variation of Old Norse words in the mede, or should it be mead names, so obviously these places were discovered at an early date.

It is good to see, even with the inevitable changes that a little interest still lingers. And we often hear the young folk saying that they would like to go out in a motor boat to have a go. If they feel so inclined we might be able to give a lead as to where they may have a chance.

Best of them all is known as "Aid's Deep" (Aith's Deep.) It is a place of great antiquity, and fish in countless numbers must have been taken there over the centuries. There is quite an interesting story about the place. It was said to have been discovered by a Viking who was out from Bergen fishing. He was caught in a gale and drifted hither and thither through the North Sea, keeping himself alive by eating fish livers. Eventually he found himself about seven miles S.E. of the Snap. Having run out of livers, and completely exhausted, he let down his line and pulled up a pair of ling. With renewed strength for a last desperate effort, he made the coast of Fetlar and landed in a geo at Aith. It was clear to his Norse kinsmen who would have been the inhabitants, that he was in a bad way. But he could converse with them and was able to describe the landmarks where he had got the fish. Tradition has it that he said "There would be mony a tired hand but never a sair heart." It can be said that the prediction, if made, was a true one. Hard pulls there were in plenty, but no lives were ever lost in coming or going.

In a short time he died and was given the traditional Viking boat burial. Visitors to the island who are looking for the spot would easily observe the large mound. We did some excavation and found a quantity of decayed nails and rather clumsy hand-wrought rooves. These seemed to tally with the descriptions of clenching used in Norway at that period. I stupidly forgot about the Lerwick Museum, where the finds could have gone, and sent them to Edinburgh.

Some of the local historians doubted the "mead" part of the story, believing that the stranger could not give a true picture of the landmarks. I fancy it would have been quite simple. He saw a long-backed hill with a steep face, with Unst well out bearing at the large holm at the east side of Fetlar. The shrewd natives would soon have figured out that he saw Vallafield at Strandbrough Ness, the other mede being the skerry at the low headland, bearing in line with a scord in the far side of the island – that is Snappa Skerry bearing in line with the Scord of the Kluster.

Part V

(*The New Shetlander*. No. 68, 1964)

The equipment of a sixern on setting out for the haaf would have comprised, among other things, a fleet of lines consisting of six "pakkies" with roughly one thousand hooks on tomes spaced at four fathoms, the fleet stretching about five miles. There were also buoys, bow-tows, bait, a fire-kettle, peats water-keg, blaand-keg, etc. The skipper would carry a little cash – not to be parted with if he could help it. He may have had to get it from the curer against such a time when the bill would be squared on pay-day. But, the younger reader may ask, "Why the cash?" Well, that was the bait money. It was part of the game to catch up with the herring boats, and strangers could hardly be expected to give gratis all the time. Herring boat skippers such as James and William Stewart were not always met with. They were the cheerful givers, delighted when surrounded by locals, and money was never thought of. The conger was rated good bait, and when sour, it was despised by dogfish, but was a delicacy for ling and cod.

Going To The Grounds

If the boats were going out to the distant ground, they would usually go in pairs, the companion boat being known as the ranksman. If it was a sailing wind the boats would sail quietly along, or the better sailer would draw ahead and get there first. But if it was calm and the boats were under oars then the going might be quite different, for it was then that the racing or "kemping" became the order of the day. This may seem today a useless waste of energy, and the crews were in for a bit of discomfort, having to sit it out in sweat-sodden clothes. But it was bred in the bone and could not be resisted. We saw much of it when boating the peats from Lambhoga. It mattered little if your boat was good or not so good, we had to have a go at it – win or lose.

On reaching the fishing grounds the usual routine would begin – setting, tiding and hauling the lines. Each member of the crew had his allotted task. One hauled, another took the fish on board with the clip or huggi-staff and unhooked them by means of a short notched stick known as the kavlin-tree. The fish would be headed and gutted by a third member, while the remaining three would andoo on the oars.

We have had several fine pictures and descriptions of the böds, or lodges, in recent numbers of this magazine. The crumbling remains of these humble abodes may still be seen above the beaches throughout the islands. There are still remains of the ones at Funzie, built in James Smith's time. With the closing down at Urie, Funzie became the chief station. Smith was manager for several years to Sir John Mitchell, and later took over on his own account. This place has a fine drying beach, but the inshore reefs placed it at a disadvantage, as the boats could not lie to moorings and had to be drawn.

It was on one of those reefs that the Funzie men lost a fine boat, the *Hawk*. This sixern was another good job from Lerwick. So let us not be stinting in a word of praise for the townsmen. Then, as now, they could roll out the galleys, at their best.

The loss of a good boat would have been a rather serious matter. A new sixern, with flooring, tofts, rudder and helm, and one pair of oars, cost £16 – a princely sum in those days. The generosity of the Shipwrecked Mariners' Society, who made grants available to members for loss or damage to boats, was a welcome windfall for the fishermen. And the sums paid out must have been considerable.

Superstitions

On thinking on the loss of boats one is reminded of some amusing stories handed down from the past. Although superstitious notions play little part in fishermen's lives today, that can hardly be said of our forefathers. Certain words when afloat, and actions on shore, meant success or failure, and were observed most carefully, even to the building of the boat itself.

It was of vital importance to guard against using "windy-wid." The planking would be carefully examined for certain light-coloured streaks in the timber, and where observed, it was at once discarded. My grandfather told me of one, Miller by name, who lived in Aith. He had some skill in woodcraft and decided to try his hand at a fourareen. It seems that he did very well for a first attempt, and just when he was receiving the praise of the lads and lasses of the township, two or three of the old fishermen came along. On giving her a quick look over they lifted their hands on horror, for the tell-tale streaks were, not in one board only, but in several. They assured the builder that she "was for it," so he thought he had better leave nothing to chance and tie her well down. But, the story goes on, "It cam some wind on the night, an she was seen no more."

Another superstition that leaves us a little bit at sea was the belief that troublesome whales or sharks were scared off by throwing overboard anything made of copper. It was a common practice to drive copper nails in the boats' keels, or one or two coins under the drawal [keel-stem scarf]. Sometimes the owskerry would be filled with water and a coin dipped in, and the water thrown in the direction of the intruder. Was it just another old notion? We just do not know. Anyway the trick was known over all the islands, and was firmly believed to have the desired effect.

Another that raises a smile was the belief that it was "ill done" to brag about the catch. A haul, of say, three score of ling would be termed "twartree." If a young lad, who hadn't learned the ropes happened to say – "That's a fine lot of fish," he would probably get a dig in the ribs with a stern "What's du sayin boy? Attend ta dee oar, an never mind what's a shott."

Trivial incidents often betokened good omens, such as when animals, especially white or grey, were seen grazing on the top of a hill or knoll that was going to be used as a mede. The ling itself was known as "hwida." Another that was counted a good sign, was when the boat was launched into the water and it tilted over to the line (starboard) side. To be quite honest, I rather liked it that way myself.

Part VI

(*The New Shetlander*. No. 69, 1964)

It has been said that necessity is the mother of invention and nowhere was this more applicable than in the lives of our forefathers. Being somewhat isolated they had to devise ways and means of doing things, both on shore and afloat.

Of course it has to be admitted that their efforts did not always win praise. One finds a spot of criticism in Hibbert's observations. He did admit that they excelled in handling their 'skiffs' in rough tidestreams, but he did not think they made such a good job of laying down the 'feals' flayed from the peat banks.

But we do give them credit for being observant and for an ingenuity that more than offset the limited means at their disposal. We have always been interested in the information handed down telling of their skill in getting in to the land from long distances, when fog could be dense for days on end, and before the magnetic needle was in general use by fishermen.

Da Moder Dy

Foremost in these arts was following in the "Moder Dy." This was, or is, a heaving motion of the sea which goes on continually moving towards the land, irrespective of wind and tide. There does not appear to be any information in ancient mariners' tales or practices, of their having used this means of finding direction, and it seems safe to assume that it was first observed by our Norse ancestors.

They depended on the sea for survival, and developed an insight that enabled them to use the elements of nature to guide them home. These arts were passed down from father to son, and those who could use them skilfully became the leaders.

We have been out on occasions with handlines at the south-east of the island, in favourable conditions, and where the mystical directive would be in motion, but we just could not detect it. So much for our powers of observation.

Other Navigational Aids

The movements overhead were also carefully noted. When the fog lifted sufficiently, the part where the Sun was would show lighter. That was termed

"Da Gludiree." They would know by the time of day where the Sun would be bearing, and this would enable them to get a rough calculation of the direction of the land, known to them by the finest of their taboo words – "Da Maana."

"Deepnin da watter" was carried out on the run in. They would know by the feel of the sinker on the bottom – "Da Dik" – if it was sandy or hard. Birds in flight, or on the water were observed. The "midder" birds out for feed for their young kept near to the land. By now it would be getting on for time to listen for "Da Brim Tud" – the sound of the sea breaking on the shore. The rest was easy.

Another method used in small boats was to tow a spar or oar astern and try to keep it running straight when on course. But we do not think this was favoured by the haaf men. Precautions were taken when lying to the lines in dense fog, against the boats being run down by passing vessels. The bow-rope was tied to the horn with a slip-knot, and the buoy bent to be ready to be dropped quickly. The oars were shipped to pull out of harm's way. The looderhorn too, was kept within easy reach, to sound a warning if a vessel's siren was heard in the vicinity. These horns, which came from Highland cattle, were purchased from Lerwick merchants. Some were better than others and those thin in the shell were best.

Weather Sense

Much has been handed down about our forebears having a good weather sense. That was not wonderful since the sea and sky was given so much thoughtful attention. A good weather prophet was of importance in those days. Here again we wonder at their uncanny foresight.

We were told by the old folks that the afternoon of 4th July, 1881, had every appearance of fine settled weather, with the "simmer dance" on the hilltops. Yet many of the older fishermen throughout the islands heard and saw what was coming several hours before the storm broke, and had a good deal of difficulty persuading the younger crews who were getting ready for sea, not to go.

A case in point was the fourareen's crew in the township of Aith. They were all set to make for the south Haaf, where they had got a good catch the day before. But they were warned by one who heard bad weather in the north-west. Luckily for them they called it off when they saw he was in earnest.

It was said that some of the men out in the boats seemed to sense that something was in the air. The swell, observed by all the crews at sea, grew as the day spent. When one of the crew of the *Spray* asked the cause of the swell, Tait, who often forgot to use the sea language, replied "The dog before his master."

The fishermen of Shetland could never be sure about the high winds. They knew that the weather in their northern waters was liable to change, but they accepted that as part of the business. No doubt they felt that if it did come, they, and a good craft to work on, would put up a good show.

Having said something about finding the land, we might add a word about early methods of catching fish, Before long lines and metal hooks came the early settlers had to fish up their "Showens fra da deep," by more primitive means. Sinkers were of stone, dressed to shape and weight, and bored to take the line. The fish-hook was a short hard-wood pin, sharp at both ends and notched in the middle where the "toam" or " skoag" was secured. The device was called a "Snarra Pin" – Norse for "snare pin." The bait was tied on with a woollen thread termed "Vaav." The thread was also used to hang the toam up by one end, at an angle, thus making it easier to be swallowed end on. When it was swallowed and weight put on, the thread broke and the pin became horizontal in the gullet or fastened in the gills.

Part VII

(*The New Shetlander.* No. 70, 1964)

When we first had in mind to contribute something to "Shetland's magazine," we felt we would like to dig into some gatherings from the past and tell the young folks something about the seafaring lives of their forefathers. If they have come across anything that has interested them, it has been worthwhile.

On jotting down something for this instalment we recalled that a few friends had mentioned that they would have liked more information about the island's skippers and their adventures. It would take a good deal of space to include them all, so we have selected a few outstanding figures.

Thomas Tait

I daresay the first mentioned will be known as he has been mentioned several times before – Thomas Tait. We have heard about how he sailed in the storm of 1881. Now let us see how he deals with a difficult situation in a calm, with the fog as thick as a hedge. They are off in the "Spray," in company with their "ranksman," the *May*. Both boats have set their lines for the night "hail," with a top tide and with Saxavord almost down when the fog descended. When getting on for hailing time, they noticed no tide on the boat. A much used strop on the "stead" [marker buoy] had chafed off and they were adrift from the lines. The skipper set up the "dykel [compass]," made his calculations, and bade them pull away. He was going to try for the inner buoy. After pulling what seemed to them a long way, he said "Sound the looderhorn." Right away they heard the *May* replying, and when they got up with her, Petrie, her skipper, reported having hailed two "pakkies." Tait took the course that Petrie was moving, then steered in the opposite direction and made an estimates of two "pakkies." He then put the helm hard over and steered west for another spell. James Hart was asked to go forrad to look out. Tait had just said that they should be about it now when James reported "buoy ahead." Good dead reckoning navigation by any standards.

Laurence Hughson

For a good second we have the man from Skerries, Laurence Hughson. Two of our forebears were part of his crew, so we heard a good deal about him. He was a man of small stature, but what he lacked in bulk he made up for in intelligence. It was told that while he and the crew were getting the boat ready he overheard two of them wondering if this "peerie body wid manage."

But he soon got his chance to show how he could manage when coming from the haaf with the reefs in. Then, by way of getting his own back, he said he would have worked her better under full sail. Laurence was reckoned a good man after that.

But it was when he was out at the "Old Fram Haaf " (20 – 25 miles) that he did what seems to us a marvellous piece of navigation. With his boat full-up with fish, in a dense fog, and all set for their seven hours pull to Funzie, he told the crew that his "dykel" was at home under his bed-head. They did not say much to this. Then he said: "But there are other ways of doing it." When he shipped the rudder he told them to pull away and to take their time but not to speak much to him. They watched him scan the water and knew what he was doing. He was taking her in by the "Moder-Dy."

The seven hours pulling seemed to them a very long time but at last "land ahead" – the Holm of Funzie – and dead on course. No wonder the crew said in a chorus: "Well done Laurence. We aye kent du wis a guid man, an so shaws on da day."

Irvine Park

Irvine Park was the man who proved to the fishermen that their old idea that a merchant seaman could not handle a sixern under full sail was far from being a true one. He went to sea in the sailing ships, and he was well on in years when he went shares in a new sixern as skipper. He was out in the storm of '81 – twenty miles to leeward. The crew suggested hanging on to the lines or trying for Skerries, but he said the boat and gear were new and they would try for home. The crew later agreed that they saw a sixern do things that night that they did not think possible. He gave her no mercy. When he brought her up to head the tide waves rushing at them, they heard the new boards cracking, And when she was drawn on the beach at Hubie, he laid his hand on the gunwale saying, "Du did weel. A'm ower weel pleased wi dee."

James Jamieson

James Jamieson, Mioness, Funzie, was another of the island's good skippers. He had a great knowledge of the fishing grounds and seemed to sense where the fish lay. He was one of those pushing men who never passed a chance. His crew were kept hard at it, but were quite happy when pay day came as they were nearly always the highest boat.

James was said to be one of the biggest and best built men who ever lived in Fetlar, and a man of prodigious strength. Some of the men rated him strongest of all Fetlar men, including even the redoubtable William Thomason. But, unlike most strong men, he would never mention his strength. If any one was bold enough to mention it to him he would say in formal English, "I do not boast or brag about the little bodily strength that has been granted me in my earthly pilgrimage." He was a pious man and a Bible scholar. Ross, the minister, went to Mioness one day to hold a house meeting and do the usual catechising. But he met more than his match that time. James ended by telling him, "We do not object to you thinking yourself a wise man, so long as you do not think we are fools." Ross did not visit Mioness for catechising after that.

The two other skippers much spoken about by the old folks were Arthur Brown, North Dale, and James Petrie, Setter. They were two of the "ocean" men and to whom the word fear was meaningless.

Another three good helmsmen were James Laurenson, Laurence Bain, and William Isbister. The latter two were at the helm in the gale of '81 and made a fine job of it. James Laurenson could make the clipper sixern, the *Queen*, get along and beat the herring boats.

But we must not leave out our finest towsman – David Hart. The words of Thomas Tait will suffice – "David knew it all, and never needed a telling."

The life may have been hard, but there was a contentment and a mutual interchange of service that seems to have made the way of life a worthwhile one.

JOHN ANDERSON OF KLUGEN

(*The New Shetlander.* No. 73, 1965)

We begin with a word of thanks to our wonderful historian, Mrs. Brown, The Bealance, Fetlar (now staying with relations in Uyeasound) for sending us the information we have been looking for about a great Fetlar seaman – John Anderson of Klugen. And we are due an apology to our worthy merchant, Mr. Robert Johnson, for our ignorance in omitting such a man as his great-great grandfather from our record of Fetlar skippers. The truth is that we have not been quite successful in obtaining information about the sixern crews who fished for the Funzie station in James Smith's time.

John Anderson was born about 1770 and occupied the croft of Klugen, which is south-west from Muckligarth. The stead of the buildings is all that is left as the stones of these croft houses were removed to build the dykes.

Our story begins when he was skipper of a smack, trading chiefly between Lerwick, Norway and Leith. The story tells that when coming from one of the northern Norwegian ports they were caught in a gale and drove before it till they brought up among ice well inside the Arctic Circle. It was midwinter and darkness around the clock up there. The crew did not understand it and though they were bewitched, and the skipper had a job to keep them cheerful. He managed it by telling them that if he could get a "glint o da seven starns" he would take them out of this. He got his "glint" and tied her up safely in Lerwick.

Another time, when crossing from Bergen, they ran into a "snifter" with wet snow. The crew came up to see how she was taking it. After watching the snow "slushing" down out of the mainsails, one of them said to the skipper, "John, dis is a bad night." He replied, "It's truly dat. An A'm tinkin aboot my peerie midderless foal under da daeks o Klugen." They thought this was a strange man who was more concerned about a foal than he was about himself.

After a period in the smack he joined the haaf men, and as skipper of a sixern was out in the great storm of July, 1832. Their adventure was truly a stirring one. In fact, we doubt if there were any to equal it in the sixern era.

Of the two Fetlar boats that did not return, Anderson's was one of them. The folks knew that he had set out for the distant grounds where the chances of survival were slim indeed. Still, they had hopes that his known courage and skill might just pull it off. But as the days and weeks passed and no returning, the crew were given up for lost.

Winter passed and spring came, and "delling" began. While the folks of Velzie were thus engaged, close to the north side of the loch they saw two men coming over the links of Tresta. An old man "lint" on his spade and said, "If John Anderson was alive I would have said at da ane nearest was him. But we ken dat canna be." But it was John Anderson, safe and sound. It is difficult to imagine what the relations felt in circumstances such as this. It must have been a wonderful homecoming.

Then came the story of their adventures in the storm. They had arrived at the Fram Haaf and were getting ready to set when the storm broke upon them with a suddenness never before seen. All they could do was to try to keep her head to it with the oars and let her fall to leeward. It was a toilsome struggle for almost three days, with all the time the spray lashing over them. At last the wind slackened, and later fell calm. Then came a chnage of wind and Anderson, who had been observing the sun's position, knew that the wind was in the wrong direction for making land and they would have to man the oars.

But they were not in good shape. They were soaked to the skin. The bread box was empty and the fire-kettle was full of water, so they could not roast their bait for food. The wind fell light and then calm, and on they rowed till they could scarcely bear the oar. Starvation was beginning to tell. The skipper heard them whispering about wanting to die. But John Anderson refused to admit defeat. He kept on trying to cheer them by saying that land couldn't be far away. And they still had water in the keg, which was something. Next day one man became delirious and died. On the following day another died, then another. The bodies were covered in the shott.

A light wind came, which Anderson made out to be from a southerly direction. Although he had tried to hide it, the valiant skipper too was losing strength. He had given his rations to weaker men and now it was telling. But the youngest of the three, when he saw that John couldn't hold the helm on his shoulder, produced a brönie [thick oatmeal biscuit] from his pocket and fed it to the skipper. His wife had slipped it into his pocket, saying, "Du better tak dis een tö: du micht need it." As he afterwards said "I keepit it for John, fur he wis wir only hopp."

Shortly afterwards land was sighted. As they drew near they looked to see if they could make it out. Then, after a time, Anderson said, "Oh less, what is come ower me dat I didna ken da Fair Isle."

On getting up to the land they came into a geo with a beach and as they were approaching the shore, they noticed a plank floating at the water's edge, in "da shurmal," as we night say. To the surprise of the others the elder man said, "Boys, if you're able, wid you help me save dis plank." They asked,

"What use is a plank ta wis?" He said, "It'll do for my coffin." Shortly after they got ashore he fell back and died.

The story doesn't go on to tell how the two survivors were found. But they were looked after by the kindly folks of Fair Isle till they got a passage in a smack going to the North Isles of Shetland in the spring of the following year. The two were put ashore in the smack's drag boat at the noost of Helliersness and made their way across Lambhoga and on to the green Links of Tresta where they were first seen.

One would think that such an experience would shorten the life of most men. But not so John Anderson. The story goes on to say that, when in his ninetieth year, he boated peats alone in a small boat from Foreland to Funzie, going two runs on a day, and furthermore that he drove the rest, i.e., flit them by ponies.

I believe our merchant's "family tree" shows a goodly portion of seafarers, and I imagine that not the least of them would be John Anderson of Klugen.

The lifting power and drive of the distinctively shaped Shetland squaresail demonstrated by Shetland Museum's replica sixern *Vaila Mae*.

Photo by Davy Cooper

Willie Nicolson

William Nicolson, R.N.R., c.1916. *Photo courtesy Mrs Maureen Cumming*

William Nicolson, born at Firth, Delting in 1874, was one of three brothers who along with their father Willam Nicolson Senior, and a cousin, survived the terrible storm in December 1900 in which four boats with their crews were lost. 22 men were drowned, leaving 15 widows, 51 orphans, and other dependents. He moved to Lerwick with his family in 1916 and worked until retirement at Freefield with Hay & Company. Towards the end of his life, he made a recording with John Graham on the subject of the winter haddock fishery, and his experiences of the storm. What follows is an edited transcript of Willie's story, from the tape now in the Shetland Archives (SA3/2/31/1,32/1). He died in 1965.

THE DELTING DISASTER, 1900

... We wir begun ta grow up, as young fellows, and wanted me faidder ta git wis a boat ta go ta da winter fishing wi. An he went down ta Lerwick and met in wi a Scalloway man. An he says, "Well, I have a boat at Scallowa; thirteen an a half feet [of keel], two year old." Faidder gud wi him ta Scallowa an bout her [*Ann*, LK 722] fae him. Sho only cost him aboot six pound ten. We got her up fae dere, we rigged oot an gud ta da fishing wi, up ta 1897.

Lowrie Goodlad hed da Malakoff. An dir wis wan day at me, an Robbie me oldest bridder, wis down, an he wis buildin aff wan o dat big twenty fower fit sixtreens. And Robbie said to him, "I wiss you'd big wis a haddock boat." "Oh," he says, "I'll soon do dat." He built her an we cam down ta drill, on da first day of October. Da last week we wir on drill sho wis ready.

Auld Lowrie says; "Whit's du gyaun ta caa dis boat?" I said; "Sho wis named lang afore sho wis built;

I'm caain her da *Happy Return* [LK 774]. We fetched her up an hit wis about tree weeks afore we got everything ready ta go ta da sea wi. We got a laen of a sail in Lerook at took da boat up. Dan da new sail cam bit it wis too heavy canvas fur da boat, far too heavy. An we condemned him. Da following year Old William Jamieson made twa jibs an mainsail fur wis, a big jib an a sma jib. An we hed a iron jibboom fur her, somethin da sam as we hed fur da racing boats . An we ran her an we hed dat class o sail upon her in 1900. She was fifteen feet on da keel, bit an awful deep boat, a six oared boat. An you couldna sail upon her aless you hed plenty o ballast intill her. You bust hae plenty o ballast atill her.

We gud aff in da morning an cam back at night. If hit wis richt wadder we wir nae time away, if we got a wind ta go an come wi. Da warst wis ida hinder end o da year, say da munt o February an dere aboot, you always hed ta go farder ta seaward for da haddocks. We hed ta go fae Firts Voe, or da head o Swinister Voe, till we got Balti Isle oot by da Snap o Fetlar an dats a long distance. An den we laid seven lines ta seaward fae dat an every wan o wir lines wis da same as da Burra Isle men's, nine buchts [of sixty fathoms each]. Da year at da disaster wis, we got da heaviest price at ever I fished haddocks at in me life. Dat wis 8/6 a hundredweight. Wir biggest shot wis 22 hundredweight o solid haddocks an we had five hundredweight o big fish, big cod, du knows, maybe an anterin o ling, dereaboots.

Some nights if we got a fine wind we wir nae time comin in. Bit if we got a nor'wast wind, aa we could do wis beat up ta da mainland o Yell an turn [beat to windward] her up alang till we got ta da Point o Burravoe, dan lay doon everything, mast, sails, every mortal thing, haul aff all wir claes an pit da oil jacket oot ower wir sark an every man tak his oar an row fur we got ta da Broch o Cuppister. Dats very near Ulstie. An dan we wid go in near da shore, set up da mast an reef her doon an lay her on ta da westert an git across ta back o Samphrey, turn her up alang da back o Samphrey till we got up ta da Helliack. Dan come in alang da head o Samphrey an cut right across fur Mossbank: sometimes, du sees, da tide wis goin ta da suddert, da string, an hit wid tak wis doon till we very nearly wir aff o da Broch, bit still we got da mainland. I mind wan night he wis nearly twal o'clock whin we got ta Mossbank. We cam ta da beach an da lights wis aa oot bit I gud up ta Pole's hoose, an I gud ta da front door an I rappit, twartree times, till wan o da servant lasses cam, sho says, "What's the matter." So I telled her. Pole he pat on his claes an cam oot an weighed da fish, fifteen or sixteen hundredweight o haddocks. An he looks at me faidder an he says, "Willie; du' ll be makin an end o deeself an an end o dis boys."

We lay in da back o Lunna Ness two times, wi a night o blind moorie fae da nor'west. Dirs a gio yundrew, atween Lunna Holm an da Taing, dey caa da Gio o Gungsta, a great big gio. An da Nicolson men an wis got in at da back o da ness, dere, we got da land. Man, we couldna do nothing at all, so we just gud in da geo an made her fast ta da clett an we lay dere – da moorie wis fit ta shock wis all night. Da first at cam abune da banks ida mornin wis me midder's uncle Robbie Sinclair, he bed in Lunna. An he cam doon upo da clett an he says, "Now, whit you'll hae ta do is try an git da sails reefed as close as you can an see if you can git in ta da aest banks o Lunna." Dats whaur da kirk is an da kirk yard an dat. So we gud, we got in dere, surely aboot eleven o'clock o day. An Peter Manson, dere, he took sae mony o wis an me Uncle Robbie Sinclair took sae mony o wis. An dey wir an Umphray man at bed ida Grind, he took sae mony o wis, du sees dey wir eleven men, six ida idder boat an five o wis. An we wir aa night dere. An dan da next day he wisna much easier, bit Peter Manson took both his Clydesdale horses doon an he took a great hawser of a rope an he pat aroond da boats an we took everything oot o dem, every mortal thing. An he bent on both da horses an he took dem right across da neck, du knows, right across till we cam ta da wast banks o Lunna, an dan he took da kerts doon an he took all da fish an all da lines an ballast an every mortal thing ower. So we ballasted dem dere an got in all oda stuff. Man, I mind we wir gotten a fine little turbot; faidder grippit him by da gills an hoved him ashore, he says; "I tink you're weel wirt dis Peter." He didna want ta tak him, no, no. Faidder says; "I tink you're well wirt it."

Dat mornin i 1900, dey wir da five o wis: me faidder an me an me auldest bridder Robbie an Ertie, me youngest bridder, an wir cousin Tammy Laurenson. I wis aboot 26 an me bridder, Robbie wis aboot 30, an Ertie wis aboot 20. Tammy Laurenson he wis 24.

Hit wis been tree weeks, just o solid gales o wind, completely above any fishing operation. We hed da lines standin baited, all in da boat, lyin in da moorings in Swinister Voe. Aboot da night it wis a gale, bit aboot four o'clock I heard me faidder risin an I heard him goin oot da door an he cam back again braaly hurriedly. An he he opened da door an says; "You'll get up; he's wan o da finest mornings ever I seen in all my life. Bit he's a most terrible crack o bretsh [swell breaking] here upo da shore."

We hed ta travel right in ower da hill o Swinister, so we took wir rodd an cam doon ta da banks an hauled oot da peerie boat an gied aff ta da haddock boat an we moored da peerie boat an gud oot. Hit wis dat little wind at da sails wir nae use ta wis, sae we hed ta pull all da way an we cam oot along da back o Linga an aroond fur da back o Fish Holm an dan da string at comes down Yell Sound, comes out an goes right east by Lunna Holm. As we cam on fur da point I said; "Faidder, dere's a boat comin past." Wan o da men sang oot; "What ship?" Me faidder says; "Oh, hits da Firth's Ness men." Anyhow we met an gud oot, an da swall wis dat heavy dat whin he gud doon we could only see da taps o his sails, an whin we gud doon he could hardly see da taps o wir sails at all. An we went oot in company till we cam aff o da Skerries o Neapoback, aff da point o Burravoe an we went oot maybe a mile or a coupla miles farder an oot dere he wis come a braw grain o wind. Da swell wis all comin in fae da south east, an da wind wis nor'west. An da nor'west wind strickin ida face o da sea, man, hit wis just da same as you'd been among a lot o baas. Da boat wis just up dis time, doon da nixt time, up da nixt time. Me faidder says; "I dunna ken. We can shut a line or two; if we shouldna git dem back hit'll not just kill wis." So we turned to an shot. Whin we wir shot fower lines me faidder lookit ta Robbie an he says; "Robbie, bend in no more lines; I'm settin no more da day." An Robbie says; "Man, du's talkin dirt, if wir no gyaun ta shut lines an dir idder men shuttin alongside o you." Faidder says; "I don't care if dey wid shut fifty fleets, I'm shootin no more." An we keepit da tidder two lines aboard. Dat Nicolson men, dey shot every span at dey hed aboard, fur dey wir clean oot o sight o wis, away ta da seaward, so dey had ta shut all dir lines. An Robbie wisna weel pleased aboot dis. Anyhow we buoyed her aff at da fower lines end an Tammy Laurenson got up da kettle. We hed a cup o tea a piece o wis an dan me faidder says; "Well, I think da best at you can do is turn tae an pit on your oilskins fur I'm goin ta tak her just as soon as ever you ir ready." Tammy Laurenson hailed da first line an me bridder Robbie hailed da second wan. Da third line I took an I began ta hail her. An ida time at I wis hailin me faidder wis rowin upo da pair o oars, in da ballast room an Tammy Laurenson wis on wan o da fore oars an me bridder Ertie on da other one. I wis standin hailin away, as fast as I could, an I happened just ta turn me head an I lookit up ta da nort. Man, I just saw fae da Horse o Burravoe right doon ta da sea just da same as you'd been covered it wi a blanket, a white blanket. An I turned aroond an I said ta me faidder; "Faidder whit is yun ... ats up yunder at da Horse o Burravoe?" Dey wir still no great wind. An he raise up upo da ballast, an he took two or tree minutes an he says; "It's da spundrift." I says, "Man, ir you mad?" Weel, I don't think at he wis gotten his two oars oot whin he struck. I can see da swall comin in fae da south east an da gale fae da nor'west an da weet snow an da sea an da spundrift an you couldna tell where you were at all.

Hughie Hughson, fae Taft, wis in da old post boat o Mossbank for a few vaiges till his new boat wis ready. Dat morning, da sea wis so heavy at dey could git hardly any ballast, becas dey couldna git ashore no wye ta git stones. Dey cam oot da last boat o da whole lot an dey shot, so dat dey cam ta lay across me uncle Lowrie Nicolson, and da Nicolson men in da big sixtreen, an wis an all. If it hed a been a fine day we coulda cried till him, he wis dat near ta wis. We tried ta hail a start bit, no, no, you couldna git her ahead at all ta git any chances o hailin lines. I sprang forward ower da tap o da boys till I got ida forehead an I started ta see if I couldna haul her ida forehead. Na, na, I could get none o her. An me faidder cried ta me, "Cut her Willie an slip her." I took da knife an cut her [the line] an Tammy Laurenson gie me da cappie [sinker] an da bow an burop [buoy and buoyrope] ta bend on afore I slippit her. An me faidder he turned round an says; "Now boys, for Lord's sake git da mast upon her as soon as ever you can or dan we'll be doon on da top o Hughie." We got da mast up an set on da stroods, but Hughie went down where he wis, because she wis a very old boat, awa maybe about forty year old. An dey wir just a lump o sea at went into her as we wir just comin right down fur da top o him bit we never seen him.

We got da sail reefed, every knot tied in at could be tied in an da peerie jib, reefed him too. We led wis on [headed] ta da nordart, now dat wis whit we did wrong, dat day, an I always told me faidder dat. Hed we a led her on ta da suddart, we wir always lightenin da sea as we got da lee o Lunna Holm an Lunna Ness; if we wir comin ta da suddart we'd awa doon aboot Brough i Whalsay, or maybe perhaps if we coulda keepit her well west, we would've gotten maybe in aboot Symbister. Bit instead o dat we led dem on ta da nordart. Da big sixtreen wis ida middle an me uncle Lowrie Nicolson wis eft, a braw bit astern, an we wir ta windward. An we all stayed an stood on a braw while bit, man, sometimes you never could take a sheet eft upon her at all. We wrought on fur aboot, an oor, an den, man, he made water [a big wave approached] away ta windward o wis: I said ta me faidder, "Faidder, deres an awful watter comin." He says; "Yes, I see." An he pat down da helm an brought her up an sho rose till him an sho cam doon bit sho never took wan drap, not wan drap for'ard upon her bit he just filled fae da ballast room an right eft, just fairly full. So whin I lookit eft I saw me faidder standin upo da shott, whaur he sat upo da peerie taft, steering, you know. An I saw da water just aboot his shooders. Robbie wis sittin wi a turn roond da halyards, an he let go an da mainsail cam doon. An da peerie jib bein for'ard, you see, slowly tirled afore da wind an sho began ta come doon an, man, I just saw da haddocks an da water just goin oot ower da side eft. I just jimpit oot o da owsing room, ower da tap o Robbie an I catched da halyards an sent da sail as high as I could get him, a weet heavy sail. An you see, wi da sail comin upon her, quick, she just made a run, an sho wis dead afore da wind dan. An it wis dan at we passed doon by da sixtreen's starn, an me uncle Lowrie Nicolson's starn, so if hit hed a been a fine day we coulda just almost shakken hands wi dem, we gud dat close ta dem. An it wis no time, you see, fae we passed doon by dem, till we lost sight o dem an it wis no time fae we left dem till da sixtreen wis lost. I gied da halyards back ta Robbie an jimpit inta da owsing room an took da shivel an I balled [threw] him ta Tammy Laurenson, an I says; "Tammy, now, if ever du did wirk i dy life, try dy best ta empty her." An we hed wan o dis peerie kegs, whit dey caad ten pot kugs, for Faroe brandy, We hed wan athin da boat fur kerryin wir water intill, an I grippit him oot o da ballast room an laid in da head o him on da kabe. I took da wan side an Tammy Laurenson took da idder side. An we never got wan single drop come aboard, till we hed her empty, sho wis as dry as a whistle.

Me faidder wis runnin her dead afore da wind an efter we got her emptied he said, "Willie, try an git up da compass, an see what coorse wir goin oot." I got da compass eft on da taft an I had ta sit an hadd her for a while afore sho stilled at you could see whaur you wir goin, dan we wir goin due east. I said, "Well, faidder, wir goin due east." "Oh dear, oh dear," he says, "Wir goin exactly oot between Skerries an Fetlar, goin right ta sea." An I said; "What ir you goin ta do now?" He says; "I'm comin no more by da wind, whadder we live or die, I'm comin no more by da wind."

So we ran fur aboot an oor or an oor an a half, fully maybe dat. I wis just sittin, an da sail wis on da sooth side an dat low at you could grip him, da sheet o da sail i your hand. I lookit oot along da leech o da sail an, man, all at wance I saw whit seemed laek da mast of a ship standin oot. I wis frightened ta say anything, I lookit again an dan actually I saw da roond dome o da lighthoose, just awa in upo da sooth side. I turned me aroond an I said, "Faidder, if you saw Skerries wid you mak fur it?" He says, "Yes, Willie, bit we'll never see hit fur wir too far ta da east." An I said, "I see da lighthoose." "Well," he says, "Where is it? " I said, "Hits bearin on da leech o da sail on da sooth side." "Well," he says, "Mak ready an tak da peerie jib, tak da reef oot o him an set da teck o him on da sooth side, take da sheets ta da port side an whin I gie you da order, wheep da mainsail aff o her. Hook da peerie jib on da traveller an send him up, fur dat'll be more as wir game ta run wi."

Many a time we hed ta tak him doon, for altagidder we could hardly run wi him, it wis too much canvas. We ran fur a braw start an dan he made a water, man, just something awful, an I said ta me faidder; "Dere's an awful o water comin." He sang oot ta Robbie; "Cut da jib aff o her Robbie." An Robbie hauled da jib doon an he ran fur, oh, easy five minutes straight right oot fae him, an dan whin he wis run sae far he he downed helm an brought her right ta da end o him. An we ran again till I wid a said we wir comin weel down on Skerries, if it hed a been a clear day we wida seen it. We ran on, an dan he cried, "Tell Robbie ta stand up an see whit part o Skerries wir comin doon on." Robbie wis fished at Skerries, you see, wi me faidder. So Robbie stood up a while an dan he turned an cried ta me faidder, he says we wir comin fur da Wast Voe, da voe ats very near ta da soothmaist end o da Wast Isle o Skerries, an its just a peerie entrance. So we carried on, till faidder says ta me, "Willie, du might'll a lookit an seen whit du tocht." I says, "Man, I have no idea aboot Skerries; I'm no been wirkin aboot Skerries at all." Bit anyhow I stud up, I lookit a start an I says; "No, no, faidder, we're never comin doon on da West Voe, wir comin in fur da Nort Mooth."

An he he says, "Well, if we come in da Nort Mooth it'll be alright as long as we can keep on da Bruray side." Dats da Aest Isle side, becase dat side is da deep water, bit on da west side dir tree baas at runs oot. Now we wir comin well doon for a skerry at lies aff o da point dere, an me faidder says, "Isn yun da Hivda Skerry, Willie?" "Yes," I said, "dats him all right." "Oh," he said, "dats all right." So he keepit her doon on da Aest Isle as much as ever he could. Bit just whin we wir comin doon' fur dis baas, man, I turned me an I sees a sea laek Ronas Hill come. I says, "Oh faidder, faidder, dere's an awful watter comin." Weel men, dat water cam an he lifted her up eft until sho stud on end, an for'ard I saw da sea just comin in ower da tap o da hinnie spot an faun doon inta da forehead. An me faidder wis wirkin da helm back an fore bit da helm wis useless because da rudder wis oot o da water. An, you see, sho wis runnin herself, as straight as if you hed led her wi a line, richt in atween da ooter baa an da second wan.

Hit wis dan at da Skerry men saw wis comin fur dir wis an old woman at wis been some wye ida West Isle, an sho cam by an said ta old William Sutherland, "Oh, Willie, Willie, what wye is du standin here, an a boat perishin ida Nort Mooth?" He says, "Dir no boat dere; dir no boats fae wis aff, an dir nane o da Delting boats aff idder, da day." Sho says, "I'm tellin dee go an git da men an go." So dey just shived on dir boots an away dey cam, aa man just slippit everything dey wir wirkin wi an dey cam right oot along da banks, right oot till dey wir very near opposite wis, an dan dey saw wis comin, so hit wis right enough. An whin dat sea lifted wis, an ran wis in atween da two baas, every man at wis watchin wis in Skerries tout at [thought] we wir finished .

Dirs a place whaur a well is, at da lighthoose gits dir water from. A boat, you see, fetches it fae dere an goes ta da lighthoose wi it. An whin we cam in aff o dere, da jib widna stand an we never tout aboot tryin da mainsail upon her for da bridge [between Bruray and Housay], you see, wis dere, an me faidder says, "Well boys, if we can't land her anywye we'll loss da mast goin under da bridge." An as we come in, dey wir a great big, tall, fellow caad John Henderson at left da crood an fled right ta da beach, an he took wan o dir burops, an tied a bit o stane ta da end o him, an he waded aff til da water wis near aboot his shooders an he fired. An, man, da stane an da bit o line just fell at da kabe whaur I wis sittin, an I grabbit a hadd o him an took twa turns aboot da kabe, an dey hauled her ashore upo da wast beach an dey lifted wis oot o her. Da men gud an got lanterns an hauled da boat ashore, took da ballast oot o her, drew her up. Hit wis five o'clock when we cam ashore, just hard dark. Bit you see da wind being norderly hit keepit da sky kinda licht so dat whin we cam up ower da green, gyaun ta da hooses, you just could see da green an dat wis aa.

John Henderson took Robbie wi him, an me faidder an me youngest bridder gud wi auld William Sutherland, an me an Tammy Laurenson we wir aside Johnny Anderson. We wir aside dem, an we cam in ta da hoose, an dey hed any amount o whisky dere, man, tons o whisky, bit do you think at dey wid gien wis a gless? Na, not wan, no, no!

Dey turned too an dey strippit wis, we wir just aa soakin, took aff every rag aff o wis an pat on dry claes upo wis an dan dey cam wi a cup o hot tea. An efter we wir gotten dis tea dan da old man gied an fetched a bottle o whisky an he gie wis just, whit you wida said wis just aboot da size of a nip o whisky an he pat in maybe aboot a half o teaspoon full o hot water in her an he gied wis no more, no, no.

He still keepit a gale all night, bit efter we gud ta bed, I just fell asleep as fast as I could. An da nixt mornin whan we gud up, Ertie still wisna very weel at all. A boat wis gyaun oot fae Skerries ta Whalsay an we sent oot a telegram wi her bit we wir hame afore dey got him. Auld William Sutherland cam in, carryin a bow [buoy] an a compass lid, twartree pieces in atween his hands an he said ta me faidder, he says, "Willie; does du ken dis things? " Faidder lookit at hit a start an he said, "Yes, I know it alright, it's me bridder-in-law's." So we just pat on [dressed], me faidder an me an Robbie an Tammy Laurenson; Ertie bed in. An we gud wi old William oot aroond da banks an whin we cam ta a place caad da Hol o da Rexter, at da back o da ness, everything belongin ta dat boat wis dere, except da hull an da sails. Now whit we thought, wis dat efter he's seen da Nicolson boat bein lost, he wis turned her an tried ta run, but you see he didn't know anything about Skerries, an on dat west side wis just wan solid ridge o baas, whit dey caa da Baas o Gewla, an he wis come in among dat baas an dat wis whaur sho wis been lost.

Dey wir no bodies ever found dere, no no. Da lighthoose men cam ower an dey axed if dey wir ony boat lost fae here, an auld William said, "No, dey

The haddock boat *Rose* at Little Linga off the east of Whalsay c.1900. The photo shows that the 24 foot long boat, probably typical of her type, was a substantial vessel suited to the winter haddock fishery.

Photo by Charles Stobie. Shetland Museum and Archives

wir none gien aff here bit dey wir been a Delting boat come here." "Weel," he says, "wir dey any more o da Delting boats off?" "Yes, yes," he says, "dir wir more off as dem." "Yes, he says, "dey wir a boat at gud doon by da Bound [Skerry], yesterday, boddam up." Apparently, dat coulda been da boat.

As we commmenced ta run fur Skerries, Johnny Laurenson wis shot closer doon on da side o Muckla Skerry; hit's aboot twa mile an a half fae Skerries. He wis shot doon alang da side o Muckla Skerry an right ta seaward. So aboot da time at we wir run maybe aboot an oor, gyaun fur Skerries, efter I saw Skerries I saw him, an said, "Faidder, I see Johnny Laurenson gien sailin ta da suddert." Noo dat man coulda been ashore in Skerries in a half an hour if he'd a squared her away an run right in yun Wast Voe, bit instead o dat he hauled her ta da wind an stud fur ta da suddert. An da stream at comes oot atween Skerries an Whalsay, whit dey caa da Skaw stream, hits just as bad as whit Bluemull Sound is. An he stud on fur I watched him; he stud on on ta suddert an westert, an crossed da Skaw stream till he just cam ida waster edge. Dan all at wance da sail went, an I turned ta me faidder an I said; "Johnny Laurenson's away."

Me Uncle Sandy Clark wis ta da suddert o Lunna Holm, atween dere an Whalsay, an he hauled his boat ta da wind an he wis goin ta mak fur Vidlin, bit da farder he cam ta da westert da more hit baet him off [to leeward], an he got among da baas in Lunnie Sound. An, of coorse, he wis born in Lunnie, so he got her oot an in among da baas till he got down ta da Soond, bit he could mak no landing fur da sea. He hed ta come doon aroond by Bunidale an right around. He got in at da back o da point an dey hed ta aandow dere till da tide run doon, an Willie Peterson [of Bunidale] gud wi dem an took dem aroond again an got dem landed i his noost.

John Blance o Mossbank, dat wis Peter Blance an John Blance, dey wir ta da suddert alongside Uncle Sandy an Peter Blance, you see, he wis an old haaf man an John Blance wis da sam. John Blance wis always sailman ta his faidder, Gilbert Blance, an Peter wis always in da boat wi his ain faidder. Dey squared her away fur Symbister, an dey run right doon, an as dey wir comin in dere he made wan lump o sea an he just filled her sae sho nearly sank.

We sailed fur hom at two o'clock on Sunday. You see, wir folk never kent; nobody knew anything, even though all da post offices wis opened an da telegraphs wis goin fae wan place ta da idder enquirin if dey saw any thing. An dey wired fae Mossbank ta da Nort o Scotland [Shipping] company ta send da *Earl* [*of Zetland*] ta Skerries ta see if dey wir any boats at Skerries, but dey widna do it aless somebody wid pay dem ta go.

Weel, as we wir comin hame troo da firt, aa da lines an da bows wis still standin, so we kent at dat two boats wis away, Johnny Laurenson an me Uncle Lowrie Nicolson. Me faidder wid never give in [accept] at da big sixtreen, a boat o twenty feet o keel, he wid never give in bit whit dey wid git ta Fetlar aa right. Bit whin we cam in fur da tail o Lunna Holm, da wind wis sudderly so we hed gien aroond da tail o Lunna Holm, an Robbie lookit up ta da Hill o Firtsness dere an he said ta me faidder, "Weel, faidder, believe du me, I'm no far wrang bit dir more away as whit we ken aboot." Faidder says, "Whit wye kens du dat?" "Weel," he says, "Sees du what people is upo da tap o Firthness Hill."

So we came in an came in an dan John Umphray saw da boat comin fae Skerries an he wired Mossbank, ta send on a message ta me midder, sho wis ida hoose herself bit dey never cam wi no message. Wir boat wis a red boddam, blue topsides an a black gunwale an da white sails; we never kutched da sails. Whin we cam by Firtsness, me Uncle Jamie Clark cam oot fae his hoose oot alang ta see whit wye me midder wis. He says, "Well, Katy, dir a boat comin, wan boat comin, sho's comin by Lunna Holm." Whin we cam up ida bearings o Linga dan she said till him, "Jamie, if du'll tak me arm an tak me ida door I'll tell dee whidder it's wir boys boat or is it no." He took her ida door an she stud an lookit a start an she says, "Yes, yes, dats wir boys boat." So we cam in athin da Voe an gud alangside da peerie boat an we moored da haddock boat an we just left her alane, you ken hit wis Sunday.

Bit dat comin ashore I never forgot or ever will forget as long as I'm alive, fur da cries o dat people, women an children an all every idder ootside person. Man, hit wis hertrendin ta hear. Me Uncle Lowrie Nicolson hed his peerie boat tied ta dir mooring an wir peerie boat wis tied ta wir mooring an at twelve o'clock on Friday he strak a flan [gust of wind] aff o da tap o da hill dere, Dales Hill, an he cam doon an da spundrift goin, an he struck dis boat o me Uncle Lowrie Nicolson, an he turned her right upo her mooth upo da water. An yit wir een wis standin alangside her an sho never gud. Dey wir an auld man i wir place an he said till a man at hed da shop doon dere, Robert Robertson: he says, "Robbie, dat men's boat is gien upon her mooth; dir away." An dat wis da boat at passed doon by da Bound boddom up; whit cam o her efter dat I canna tell you.

Seven boats left Mossbank dat morning; dir wis fower o wis ta da nordert an tree ta da suddert, dat wis Johnny Laurenson an Sandy Clark an Peter Blance ta da suddert o Lunna Holm. Dan dey wir wis an da Nicolson men an Hughie Hughson an me Uncle Lowrie Nicolson ta da nordert. Oot o dat dey wir just wis an me Uncle Sandy Clark an Peter Blance, dat wis all at cam back, tree boats. Dey wir 22 men lost an dey wir just wan man's body fun oot o da whole load o dat. Big Willie Nicolson, dat wis a cousin o me faidder's; da Mid Yell men hailed his body aboot tree or fower weeks efter. Me faidder an me gud ta Mid Yell ta see if we could identify him. Bit hit wis him alright.

Shetland Museum's replica sixern *Vaila Mae*. *Photo by Davy Cooper*